סֵפֶר הַמּוֹלָדוֹת וְהַתְּקוּפוֹת

רבי אברהם אבן-עזרא

The Book of Nativities And Revolutions

by
Rabbi Avraham Ibn Ezra

Edited from Hebrew Manuscripts,
Translated and Annotated
by Meira B. Epstein

Edited with Additional Annotations
From the Latin Translation
by Robert Hand

ARHAT Publications

ACKNOWLEDGMENTS

Many thanks to the Jewish Theological Seminary Library, Rare Books and Manuscripts Department in New York, Biblioteca Apostolica Vaticana, Rome, Bibliothèque nationale de France, Conservateur des manuscrits, Paris, Bayerische Staatsbibliothek, München, and the Oxford Bodleian Library, Department of Oriental Collections, for their kind permission to use copies of their manuscripts for the purpose of research, text comparison and translation. Also thanks to IMHM – the Institute of Microfilmed Hebrew Manuscripts, Jewish National and University Library, Jerusalem, for facilitating the acquisition of microfilm copies of the manuscripts.

Table of Contents

Rabbi Avraham Ben Meir Ibn Ezra (1089-1164) was a renowned Jewish scholar, whose accomplishments and prolific writing encompassed Biblical exegeses, Hebrew grammar, personal, national and liturgical poetry, philosophy, mathematics, geometry, astronomy and astrology. In mainstream Judaism he is known mainly for his Bible commentary as well as his poetry, whereas to the medieval Christian European world he became known through his astrological and scientific works.

Ibn Ezra was born in Tudela, Spain, but spent most of his adult life wandering throughout the Jewish communities in southern Spain, North Africa, Italy, France and England. It was Italy and France (about 1140 – 1160) where he wrote his astrological works. For detailed information about his life and his work see my article in *The Astrology Book - The Encyclopedia of Heavenly Influences,*[1] and also in *www.bear-star.com.* A list of his works with brief descriptions is also given in Appendix A. Also see bibliography

The Book of Nativities and Revolutions (Sefer Ha 'Moladot Ve 'ha 'Tequfot ספר המולדות והתקופות) is the third publication in the series of English translations of Avraham Ibn Ezra's astrological works. The other two are *The Beginning of Wisdom (Reshit Hokhma,* ראשית חכמה), 1998, and *The Book of Reasons (Sefer Ha 'Te 'amim,* ספר הטעמים), 1994. Together, these three, written by Ibn Ezra in this sequence, make one integral body of the basic astrological doctrine: Introduction of fundamentals, further theoretical explanations and the application to the individual birth chart.

About the HebrewTitle: *Sefer Ha 'Moladot Ve 'ha 'Tequfot*
ספר המולדות והתקופות

In all the Hebrew manuscripts of this work the title is *'Moladot'* or *'Sefer Ha 'Moladot' - The Book of Nativities* - not *'Moladot'* and *'Tequfot'*. Yet, scholars seem to treat the *'Tequfot'* section as a distinct second part. Also,

---

[1] *The Astrology Book – The Encyclopedia of Heavenly Influences*, edited by James R. Lewis, 2nd edition (Canton MI: Invisible Ink Press, 2003).

the manuscripts that contain this section are considered the full, long version.

'*Moladot*' means 'nativities' and refers to birth chart configurations. '*Tequfot*' essentially means periods, and in the calendar it refers to cycles of time and seasons. In the astrological context, it specifically refers to the system of annual revolutions as well as other astrological cycles. The root of '*tequfot*' means to go around, to circumambulate.

The word 'revolution' is also found in the title of the Latin translation. See Robert Hand's Editorial Notes.

For shorthand convenience, henceforth it will be referred to in this book as *Moladot*.

The Text and the Manuscripts

As of this publication, no critical edition of *Moladot* is available yet. This translation was primarily prepared from a microfilm copy of the manuscript in the Vatican Library, thoroughly edited using four additional manuscripts – three from the Oxford Bodleian Library and one from Bibliothèque nationale, Paris – all on microfilm. Peter of Abano's Latin translation was also used for comparison and cross-reference by Robert Hand, the editor. See Robert Hand's Editorial Notes.

The Hebrew Manuscripts:

Biblioteca Apostolica Vaticana, codex 390 Palat. Ebr. 1436. (henceforth BAV390)

Oxford Bodleian, MS Mich. 39, (OX 2023 Cat. Neu) 1813 (henceforth OX39)

Oxford Bodleian, Opp. Add. Qu. 160 (OX 2518 Cat. Neu) 1367 (henceforth OX160)

Oxford Bodleian, Opp. 707 (OX 2025 Cat.Neu) 1410 (henceforth OX707)

Paris, Bibliothèque nationale heb. 1056 (henceforth PAR1056)

BAV390 was obtained by me in 1997. The "lead" was information found in Yehuda Leib Fleischer's introduction to his Hebrew edition of Ibn

Ezra's *The Book of The World – Sefer Ha'Olam* (ספר העולם)
(Timishurara, Romania: 1937). This manuscript is also mentioned in his
introduction to his publication of *Sefer Ha'Mivharim* (ספר המבחרים) –
The Book of Elections (Clui, Romania:1939). Fleischer lists as his source
a photocopy, obtained for him by a colleague in 1931 from the Vatican
Library, codex 390 Palat. Ebr. 1436. He also lists the other texts contained
in this codex, which include *Moladot*.

The other three MSS are found on microfilm at JTS - the Jewish
Theological Seminary Library in New York, and the microfilm of the
Paris MS was obtained from IMHM - the Institute of Microfilmed Hebrew
Manuscripts, Jewish National and University Library, Jerusalem.

A preliminary survey of the dates of 31 available manuscripts which
contain *Moladot*, as listed in the online catalogue of IMHM, shows the
following: Two early MSS are dated 1367 and 1410. Two MSS are dated
1300's-1400's. The bulk of them are dated either 1400's or 1400's-1500's
and seven range from 1600's to 1800's. Some of the MSS are described as
'longer version' and one is said to be the same as MS390.

Based on my editing of the above four MSS, with additional personal
inspection of the physical MSS at JTS – Jewish Theological Seminary,
New York (MS 2629, MS 2623, MS 2625, MS 2558), as well as this
initial survey, it is safe to assume that BAV390, which is among the early
ones (1436) contains the complete work of *Moladot*.

With minor exceptions, the study of the manuscripts shows very high
degree of identity with BAV390. They can all be described as 'the full
version' since they all include the second part of *Tequfot*. For a description
of the differences found, see below: "On Editing the Manuscript and On
the Translation."

For detailed descriptions of Ibn Ezra's astrological works see
Bibliography.

Editing the Manuscript

The microfilmed manuscript of BAV390 was first printed in hard copy
and then, using a Hebrew word processor, was typed into a computer file
matching as closely as possible its physical appearance on the image of
the original page. This first step immediately required some word and
letter resolution due to blurring and corruption of the text, as well as
similarity between letters. Then it was further edited into a second file for
punctuation, chapter headings and final resolution of all the words and
phrases.

The third step was editing the work using the other manuscripts. This was done in great detail, examining every difference, great or small. Attention was paid to differences in contents, orthography, spelling, grammar and style. The result is something close to a critical edition of the text. In most cases problematic text was clearly resolved when two or more manuscripts agreed.

Types of Differences Among the Source Manuscripts:

Missing text: Occasional missing phrases were noted. This was more prevalent in OX707. Applicable phrases missing in BAV390 were supplemented from the other texts.

Word order: Hebrew allows rearranging parts of the sentence without loss of meaning. Because of this flexibility some copyists may have taken literary liberty or may have tried to "improve" the text. After generations of copying, often done by scribes who might not have known astrology, some of the contents became corrupt. Quite often the sentences had to be reread and rearranged to make out the astrological sense. Many of these variations, in my opinion, are stylistic only and do not constitute a significant difference in version.

Gender: Occasionally the gender inflection is attributed to the wrong noun, verb or adjective, resulting in an erroneous meaning.

Numbers and Orthography: Numbers are written in letters. Similarity of letter shape leads to obvious errors. Examples are: ‫ ס - מ ,ר - ד ,ב - כ‬, ‫ ה - ת - ח ,ג - כ ,ז - ו - נ‬ .

Abbreviations: A typical need for word resolution came from the frequent use of abbreviations, which is characteristic of rabbinical writing, as well as from the concise nature of the Hebrew language. Such abbreviations come either as acronyms, or as the first one or more letters of the word followed by an apostrophe.

Punctuation: Punctuation is practically nonexistent. Occasionally it is noticed, and sparsely and inconsistently inserted by the copyist. The same is true for paragraph division. Chapter headings are emphasized and actually appear to be the same across all manuscripts.

Note: OX707 has numerous notes on the page margin and inside the text above the lines, which consist of correction to the main body of the text and supplementing the missing sections. This is written by a different hand in a later style, and seems to be the work of an anonymous "editor," who knew astrology and also had in front of him a good copy of the work. In most cases these agree with BAV390.

Resolving the Differences:

I can safely state that no amount of knowledge of the older rabbinical style and Hebrew grammar is sufficient by itself. It is quite obvious that knowledge of ancient and classical astrological doctrines and familiarity with Ibn Ezra's sources are essential to the process. This also has helped in deciding whether a difference was important and meaningful, or merely stylistic.

The punctuation, added by myself, also turned out to be a critical task since in many cases it determined the correct meaning and the understanding of the text. The division into paragraphs is also not in the original text and was done here based on the topics. The main chapter headings from the original text appear in this translation in bold capital letters. The pagination of the original manuscript (BAV390) has been preserved inside square brackets [1], [2]. etc.

In general, all of the issues were resolved based on the astrological context and annotated extensively. The careful analysis of all the above led to the final edited text that was used for this translation. It must be added that the process of the translation itself further helped in finalizing the interpretations of some of the places that remained ambiguous after the editing.

The Translation

As mentioned previously cross-reference with the Latin translation by Peter of Abano (1250-ca.1315) was made by Robert Hand, the editor. This process also helped in resolving some difficult places in the text. See more information in Hand's Editorial Notes.

As in the previous translations, a typical situation is the tendency of the Hebrew language to phrase sentences in the active voice, when in English it might be expressed in the passive voice. In most cases I chose to keep the original active voice and stay as close as possible to the sentence structure, in order to preserve the tone of the original text as much as possible.

Phrases in square brackets [ ] were added to the text in two situations: One, to help the syntax and structure of the sentence for the purpose of making it more English-like and fluent for the reader. Two, when the astrological contents needed resolution, in which case my own judgment and astrological knowledge were applied. In all cases, the sentence faithfully conforms to the original which can be followed if you let your eye skip over the text in the brackets.

Phrases in parentheses ( ) are a short paraphrase, explanation or other form of information that I felt was appropriate at the spot, rather than in a footnote.

Where necessary, or possible, annotated cross reference is made to Ibn Ezra's other books, as well as his numerous other sources, such as Dorotheus, and Ptolemy's *Tetrabiblos*, whom he quotes regularly. Much more can be done in this regard, which would constitute a separate research project by itself.

The Contents

Part One – Moladot is primarily about the signification of the astrological houses in the nativity, with additional discussions of various issues that pertain to those houses, as well as references to discussions in his previous books.

By way of introduction, the book starts out with a general treatise on a question which astrological doctrine has always had to grapple with, that is, the issue of the fate of the individual within that of the collective, as it appears at times of great catastrophes. The question is always whether all the people who perish in a collective disaster have death indicated in their charts all at the same time. Another issue touched upon is astrology's answer to the famous question of Nature vs. Nurture, i.e., "how does the social and natural environment the native is born into effect the potential of the nativity?" See more on that below under "Where Astrology Meets

Religion and Philosophy."

The second part of the introduction deals with the methods of chart rectification, evaluating Ptolemy's approach, also known as the Animodar, as well as the method based on the moment of conception, later known as the "Trutine of Hermes."

The houses are already discussed in *The Beginning of Wisdom*, but here they are dealt with in a more complex way. The chapter on the First House also deals with the length of life of the native, and the chapter on the Fourth House also contains a discussion on the length of life of the native's parents.

A point of interest is his treatment of house/sign interrelationships. In addition to the traditional listing of house significations, Ibn Ezra shows how specific patterns of house/sign overlay, as determined by the rising sign, create their own built-in meaning, regardless of the condition of the ruling planets.

Part Two – Tequfot is a discussion on the method of calculating the annual revolution, as well as the months and the days for the method of the annual profection. Under *'The Days'* he also mentions the evaluation of what is known as Planetary Hours (the planetary rulers of the days of the week and hours of the day.) These topics briefly appear in *The Beginning of Wisdom*. Here, Ibn Ezra also provides guidelines for interpretation of the annual revolution chart.

Part Three – Elections. This last section is a short treatise that provides some considerations on the topic of elections - the astrological doctrine of electing an auspicious time to start an important endeavor. It is interesting to note that Ibn Ezra wrote *The Book of Elections (Sefer ha'Mivharim* ספר המבחרים) immediately after *Moladot*.

Where Astrology Meets Religion and Philosophy

The book opens with a high-level statement of his philosophical thought which cuts to the core of a fundamental technical, and ultimately metaphysical issue that astrology raises, and that is the fate of the individual within the collective.

The question of the *general rule versus the particular individual case* is found in Jewish sources in numerous places, Talmudic and others, where there is a need to define the law, explain its origin and deal with exceptions. The debates are on the relationship between the specific case and the general rule that covers it. Most of the time, the general rule is derived from the commonality of the detail. On the other hand, by virtue of being an inclusive principle that contains the essence of the law and which often originates in the Torah, it can also overrule the detail.

Ibn Ezra combines these principles with the astrological doctrine by using Hebrew phrases that contain the words *'klal'* (כלל) meaning 'general', and *'prat'* (פרט) meaning an individual, single item or specific case. These appear in the text in phrases such as:

דיני הכללים יבטלו הפרטים
כח זה הפרט לא יוכל לבטל הכלל
הפרט לא יוכל לבטל הכלל
והדרך הששית מפאת המלך כי כחו ככח כלל
כי התולדת היא פרט והכלל שבחר לא יועילנו

All of these state that the general law that encompasses all situations overrides the individual case, with some qualifications, as can be seen in the text.

'Klal' (כלל) also refers to 'the whole', and is also used to denote 'the public, the collective, the group, the community'. The verb 'to include' is derived from it. *'Prat'* (פרט) by contrast, refers to the individual person within the group.

In astrology under the heading of 'Mundane', groups of people, such as nations, countries, organizations and so on, are considered to be integral entities that have their own inception chart and collective destiny. Ibn Ezra addresses the question of what happens when there is a contradiction between the indications of the chart of the individual and that of the collective with regard to "good times" versus "bad times." His unambiguous conclusion is that the general prevails over the individual, and the variations and levels of intensity are relative to the destiny of the group.

In a similar hierarchical manner he also builds his arguments from the general to the particular, starting from the level of peoples and nations, through kingdoms, through social and natural environments, down to the individual level where a person must exercise knowledge, wisdom and common sense. And when there are no more answers, there is always the faith in God's providence and the belief in the power of the soul to find the necessary wisdom and knowledge that is right for the circumstance. When it comes to this last resort, he speaks of 'the power of the *Neshamah*, the soul, which is the power of wisdom and knowledge' (כח הנשמה וכחה היא החכמה). In his matter-of-fact style Ibn Ezra gives another reason for the need for faith, saying that astrologers sometimes err in judgment, and therefore, the righteous believer is more protected than the one educated in the knowledge of the signs, since the believer is empowered by the soul.

Ibn Ezra picks up this topic again, at the beginning of his *Sefer ha'Mivharim – The Book of Elections*, which was written immediately after *Moladot*. He repeats the statement about the *Neshamah Elyona* (נשמה עליונה) – the highest soul, yet with emphasized qualification, saying that it has the power to cancel only some of the details, increasing or decreasing the indications of the stars, but not completely cancel what the *klal* – the general overruling power – indicates.

Ibn Ezra was a deeply religious person. In a book called *Yesod Mora* – יסוד מורא (meaning:"The Foundation of Awe") he advocates the study of astrology as well as the other sciences – all for the ultimate purpose of the profound knowledge of God through better understanding of the physical sciences, astrology, the Torah and the Talmud, in this order, since each one necessitates the other.

In that treatise he lays down the classical doctrine of the three parts of the soul:

- *The Soul (Nefesh, נפש)* is the vegetative lower part, which is shared with animals and experiences the physical, bodily needs and sensations – desire, hunger, pain, etc.
- *Spirit (Ru'akh, רוח)* is the middle part, also in the physical body and shared with animals. It causes movement and motion. It is the mind, the capacity for understanding and the character or personality.
- *The Neshamah Elyona, נשמה עליונה – The Highest Neshamah – "the highest soul"* – is the part that is connected with God. It is of the divine and dwells in humans only. The *'Neshamah'* is the part that returns to God after the death of the body. It is above the influence of the stars, unaffected by the worldly, sublunar conditions, i.e., the circumstances of the nativity. All three parts, *Nefesh, Ruach, Neshamah*, need each other and work together. The *Nefesh* seeks worldly satisfaction of the body. The *Ru'akh* is in the middle, like a

mediator, and the *Neshamah* seeks the knowledge of the workings of God. It is the *Neshamah* that travels up to the heavens and brings back wisdom and knowledge.

To the best of my knowledge, *'Neshamah'* does not have an equivalent in the English language.[1] Both *Ru'akh* and *Neshamah* relate to wind and air, as does 'spirit'. *Ru'akh* (רוח) is also wind and *Neshamah* is related to *neshimah* (נשימה) – breathing.[2]

Ibn Ezra's work represents the intellectual spirit of his time in many ways, by combining the philosophical and the religious impulse with the scientific exploration. Astrology occupies a unique place since it stands at the threshold between these, and by definition of its doctrine confronts the seeker with the hard questions of predetermination versus free will, as well as the role and merit of faith and religious virtue. Ibn Ezra was a deeply religious Jew but at the same time he never wavered from the truth of astrology. This is abundantly clear in his astrological writing as well as in his personal poetry. More of this in the future.

Meira B. Epstein
New York, 2008

---

[1] Although undoubtedly different in details, this doctrine closely parallels the western medieval doctrine of the *vegetative, animal,* and *intellective* souls derived from Aristotle's *De anima* by way of medieval Arabic philosophy. [RH]

[2] *Spiritus* in Latin also means 'wind' and is related to our word 'respiration'. [RH]

The Latin Text: Throughout this translation of *The Book of Nativities and Revolutions* there are frequent references made to the Latin translation of this text. The particular edition that we have used here is the edition printed by Peter Liechtenstein in Venice in 1507. The copy that was employed is from an online display of the complete work by Bibliothèque nationale at http://gallica.bnf.fr/. The full titlepage inscription is as follows:

> Abrahe Avenaris Judei Astrologi peritissimi in re iudiciali opera ab excellentissimo Philosopho Petro de Abano post accuratam castigationem in latinum traducta.

According to Raphael Levy[1] this is a translation from the Old French of Hagin the Jew into Latin, and according to Levy this translation has many problems. However, as Meira Epstein went though the original Hebrew of the Vatican Library manuscript (BAV390), she and I both agreed that it would be good to compare the translation from the Hebrew with one of the Latin translations, and this is the edition that was available to us. Despite the problems of this Latin translation, at the beginning of this project we had only the above Hebrew manuscript to serve as the basis for the translation; therefore it was decided that I would go through the Latin version point by point and compare it to the translation from the Hebrew. As it turned out near the end of this project, Meira Epstein turned up quite a number of additional Hebrew manuscripts which made her translation much less dependent upon BAV390. Despite this we both decided to leave the references to this Latin version in the notes to the text. Even with all of the corrective material from the additional Hebrew manuscripts, there were still a few occasions where the Latin text elucidated or even corrected the translation obtained from the Hebrew. Also, there were times when the Hebrew reading showed us something sufficiently unusual that it was good to have agreement from the Latin to support the reading from the Hebrew. For a complete discussion of the issues concerning the

---

[1] Raphael Levy, *The Astrological Works of Ibn Ezra* (Baltimore, MD: Johns Hopkins Press, 1927), 32-46. [RH]

Hebrew manuscripts please see the section of Meira Epstein's Introduction beginning on page viii.

The Pluses and Minuses of the Latin Text: The main advantage that the Latin text offers is that it likely represents a completely different manuscript lineage than any of the surviving Hebrew manuscripts. The translation from Old French to Latin was made in or about 1293 CE. The printed edition was compiled from one or more manuscripts of the Latin in 1485 in Venice. Our 1507 edition was probably based on the 1485 edition. Obviously there has been no further evolution of the text since the printing in 1507.

The main disadvantages of the Latin text for our purpose are two: first, the translation itself is of somewhat questionable merit (see Levy); second, it is unlikely that the 1485 edition was assembled from anything resembling a critical text. Add to that errors in typesetting, and one can easily see how the Latin text does not always prove to be a help in understanding the Hebrew. As the reader will see in perusing the notes regarding the Latin text, quite a number of obvious typographical errors were encountered.

As mentioned elsewhere in the notes, when the Latin text is quoted at length, the original punctuation has been left intact. Most especially the reader should note that colons [:] in this edition have been used in a manner more like our commas, and periods [.] often do not properly denote the end of sentences. The English translations reflect the intent of the text, not the punctuation used in the 1507 edition. Otherwise, the only change I have made in the Latin text is to expand abbreviations and to change the uses of the letters 'u' and 'v' to reflect the modern practice.

Footnotes: Notes have been provided by both Meira Epstein and myself. If there is no notation in a note, the note is from Meira Epstein. If the note was provided by myself, there will be the notation [RH] in the note. Notes which were started by myself and added to by Meira Epstein will contain [MBE].

THE BOOK OF NATIVITIES AND REVOLUTIONS

[Introductory Matters: Overall Considerations Before Judgment][1]

Avraham, the Spaniard,[2] said: Anyone who is learned in the science of the judgment of the signs[3] and does not know the higher wisdom, there will be times when his judgments will be false, for he has not been cautious of the things that ought to be properly avoided. As a rule, he said that judgments for the general group void the judgment for the individual (person),[4] and of these I shall mention eight ways.

The first way is that he must know of which nation the native is. [2] For [example,] if the nativity is of an Israelite and the astrologer has seen in the constellation of the stars of his nativity that the native should become a king, it is not proper to judge so, because it has already been made clear from the Great Conjunction, which is the conjunction of Saturn and Jupiter, that his nation would be in exile.[5] Thus, this individual influence cannot cancel the general one, so it is proper to judge that the native will be with kings, be involved with them and deal with them but he will not be a king himself. Similarly, if [one] found Saturn in an Israelite nativity in the Ninth House, it will not indicate that the faith of

---

[1] Titles in square brackets [] are not in original manuscripts. [RH].

[2] Referring to himself.

[3] In the traditional Jewish literature the word for 'sign' (*Mazal,* מזל) is often used as a general term for the total constellation of the astrological chart, and its various configurations.

[4] See translator's introduction, under the heading of "Where Astrology Meets Religion and Philosophy."

[5] Therefore, having no sovereignty nor a sovereign. [Additional by RH.] According to Abu Ma'shar, the Great Conjunctions of Jupiter and Saturn describe what happens to religions and dynasties. Traditionally the most important of these occur every 960 years (the actual figure being less than that). From the ingress charts which precede these conjunctions one was supposed to be able to tell what religions and dynasties were going to be dominant or not dominant in any of these periods. Ibn Ezra is clearly taking the long view here and saying that if one were to perceive from such a chart that Jews were going to be a down-trodden religion in exile, with no state, (a realistic view in his lifetime), then forecasting royal status for Jewish individuals would be inappropriate regardless of the merits of the chart. The indications of the longer range cycle charts subsume any indication of a mere natal chart. See Abu Ma'shar, *On Historical Astrology: The Book of Religions and Dynasties (on the Great Conjunctions),* translated by Charles Burnett & Keiji Yamamoto (Leiden, Boston: Brill, 2000), passim.

the native in his religion is improper; only in the Moslem nativities will it be so.

The second way is to judge from the regions [of the earth], for [if] one [is] born in the land of Kush,[1] even if Venus is with the Moon in the rising degree, we will not judge that the native will be handsome and white compared to the people in other regions but he will be so only [relatively] compared to the appearance of the people of his [own] region. Similarly, if the ruler of the nativity is Mercury, we will not judge that he will be knowledgeable in all kinds of science; for it is not possible [for one] to be learned in the land of Kush because of the excessive heat of the Sun, and therefore his nature will not be forthright (properly manifest) and we will only judge that he will be intelligent compared to the people of his own locality.

The third way is the rule that comes from the [effect of the] Great Conjunction on each country. Thus, if within the influence of the Conjunction upon the nations the sword[2] is supposed to befall a certain nation, even if many of those of those born in it do not have an indication of death by sword in their nativities, when the time [for war] for that country comes, they will all be killed.

The fourth way is [judged] from the revolution[3] of the world. If it shows in the [general] revolution that a disease will occur in a certain country, even if a nativity of a person in that country does not have [an indication] that he will be sick that year, that disease will happen to him since the individual indication will not cancel [that of] the general.

The fifth way is from the [influence of] the family. For, if two are born at the same moment in the same country,[4] and one is [3] the son of a

---

[1] Kush was a name commonly used to designate Nubia (now Sudan) in Africa. More technically it was the southern province of Nubia at a time when it was ruled by Egypt in the 15th century B.C.E. [RH]

[2] War. Also see previous note on the Great Conjunctions.

[3] The phrase is 'The period of the world' – *'Tkufat Ha'Olam'* (העולם תקופת). *'Tkufa* - period' comes from the Hebrew verb that means to go around, to circumscribe, to revolve around. It is also used in calendar terms as 'the period of the year, or of the month', to denote the completion of the period. In this astrological context it is a reference to the 'Annual revolution of the Sun'. [Additional by RH] The phrase "revolution of the world" is a standard medieval phrase for the chart erected each year at the exact moment of the vernal equinox.

[4] Obviously he means 'place', thus having the same chart.

minister[1] and the other is the son of a lowly servant, and it is within the influence of the nativity to rise to a high rank and great authority, the son of the minister will become king and the son of the servant will become a merchant.

The sixth way is [judged] from the [nativity of the] king for that nativity's influence is like the influence of [a chart that affects] the general group. So if [it is indicated] in the king's nativity that he will go to war, then he will send to war many people in none of whose nativities there is an indication of [that individual's] moving away from his [own] place.

The seventh way is from the [laws of] nature. For if a man goes in a ship in the cold season at sea and the sea becomes stormy, even if he places Jupiter and Venus, which are the benefic planets, in the rising degree, he will not be saved[2] for the [general] nature is the [overriding rule] and the specific [chart] that he elected would not benefit him. Similarly, if a thousand people die at sea in one ship, you will not find in everyone's nativity that he would die that year, although in each of their nativities it will be found that one of the lords of life has come to a dangerous place (but not necessarily fatal), and if he had not been at sea, which is a dangerous place, only little harm would befall him and he would be saved.

The eighth way is [judged] from the influence of the soul and its power[, which] is wisdom.[3] For if a native is knowledgeable in the science of the signs and he sees in his annual revolution that he will become ill due to heat at a certain time when Mars enters his rising degree, then, if prior to the onset of the illness he avoids every hot food, and drinks beverages to cool his body, his bodily constitution will be re-balanced when Mars enters his rising degree.[4]

And so, [for] the one who has faith in God with all his heart God will turn things around and change circumstances to save him from every harm [indicated] in his nativity. Therefore, there is no doubt that the righteous person is more protected than the one knowledgeable in the judgment of

---

[1] In the political or official sense of the word 'minister.' [RH]

[2] This refers to an electional chart drawn up for setting out on a journey.

[3] The word is 'hokhma' (החכמה), which means 'wisdom' but is also used in older Hebrew to denote science, learning and knowledge.

[4] This is medieval medical astrology: The idea here is to maintain a balance by cooling down the body in anticipation of the increased heat that will come from Mars.

the signs for at times the latter will be erroneous in judgments, as the scripture says "and maketh diviners mad,"[1] so happy is the one whose heart is whole with God.

After having said these things I shall mention what [4] the ancients have tried, and because there are numerous books in the science of the signs and [in them] there are things that reason will refute, and there is a dispute in the judgments of the signs, I must mention in this book every clear thing that the ancients agreed on and [which] I have tried many times.

THE EQUATION[2] OF THE NATIVITY

[Rectification – the Nimodar]

Ptolemy said that we could know the rising degree from his method of equation which in the Persian language is called Nimodar, and he

---

[1] "וקוסמים יהולל" from Isaiah 44:25: "That frustrateth the tokens of the liars and maketh diviners mad; that turneth wise men backward, and maketh their knowledge foolish."

[2] The Hebrew title is 'moznei hamolad' (מאזני המולד) which can be interpreted as 'the scales of the nativity' or 'the balance of the nativity', and refers to a discussion of a doctrine of chart rectification also known as Animodar. See Tetrabiblos, book III chapter III. See Claudius Ptolemy, Ptolemy's Tetrabiblos, translated by J. M. Ashmand (Chicago: Aries Press, 1933), 74-75. All references to this edition of this translation will be referred to as Ashmand. [Additional by RH] The word for balance is translated into Latin as aequatio from which we get the word "equation." This is a word often used in the context of computing or calculating. Checking the Oxford English dictionary we also find the following reference under "equation":

II. Reduction to a normal value or position.
3. a. Astr. The action of adding to or subtracting from any result of observation or calculation such a quantity as will compensate for a known cause of irregularity or error. Chiefly concr. the quantity added or subtracted for this purpose.

Also, in most old languages, 'equate' and 'equation' are simply the equivalent of "compute/computation" or "calculate/calculation."

4

mentioned it in the book *The Four Chapters*,[1] also in the *Book of the Tree*[2] and also in the book *The Small Magician*.[3] And so he said: We shall look to see if the nativity was between the time of the conjunction of the luminaries and their opposition, and we shall seek the degree of the conjunction that preceded the birth[4] and we shall seek the ruler of that degree. And we shall seek this from the ruler of the domicile, the ruler of the exaltation, the ruler of the triplicity, the ruler of the bound, and the ruler of the face;[5] and we shall seek the one that has the most dominion

---

[1] Ptolemy's *Tetrabiblos*. The phrase is *"Arba'a She'arim"* (ארבעה שערים), and is consistently used by Ibn Ezra to denote this book. *"She'arim"* (plural of *"sha'ar"*, literally meaning 'gate') is used in older Hebrew to mean chapters in a book.

[2] Probably *The Centiloquy*, one hundred aphorisms attributed to Ptolemy. In other places Ibn Ezra calls it *The Book of Fruit*. Ashmand refers to it as the *Fruit of the Tetrabiblos*. In the footnote, Ashmand also acknowledges the question of the authorship of this book. Note that there is no reference to the Animodar method in the *Centiloquy* as published in Ashmand's translation of the *Tetrabiblos*. It is in the main body of the text in Book III. (Ashmand, 153n, 74-75).

[3] Unidentified. [Additional by RH] However, it could be any one of several magical works attributed spuriously to Ptolemy in the medieval world. See Francis J. Carmody, *Arabic Astronomical and Astrological Sciences in Latin Translation* (Berkeley, CA: University of California Press, 1956), 19-20.

[4] In Book III Chapter III Ptolemy says ". . . the new or full Moon, whichever it may be, that may take place next before the time of parturition, must be observed: and, if a new Moon, it will be necessary to mark exactly the degree of the conjunction of the two luminaries; but, if a full Moon, the degree of the luminary only which may be above the earth during the parturition." Ashmand,, 74.

[5] The Hebrew word is *'panim'* (פנים) which means 'face'. However, in earlier sources there is a great deal of confusion about this mode of rulership. In the corresponding section of the *Tetrabiblos*, (book III, chapter III), under the title "The Degree Ascending," the text calls it 'phase or configuration.' Ashmand's footnote says: "Phase or configuration. Or, holding some authorized aspect to the degree in question." (Ashmand, 74) In R. Schmidt's translation the footnote says: "This is a troublesome expression. Phase almost certainly refers to solar phase. But it is not clear whether configuration refers to aspect or is merely another way of describing phase. See Claudius Ptolemy, *Tetrabiblos Book III*, translated by Robert Schmidt (Berkeley Springs, WV: Golden Hind Press), 8. In Ptolemy's *Phases of the Fixed Stars* phase is itself defined as a special configuration involving the planet, sun and horizon." (Claudius Ptolemy, *Phases of the Fixed Stars*, translated by Robert Schmidt (Berkeley Springs, WV: Golden Hind Press), xiii-xiv.

and compute its place in the wheel of the signs in the tables of

---

In the *Tetrabiblos*, book I, chapter XXVI, under the title "Faces, Chariots, And Other Similar Attributes Of The Planets," we find: ". . . There are also, however, further peculiarities ascribed to the planets. Each is said to be in its *proper face*, when the aspect it holds to the Sun, or Moon, is similar to that which its own house bears to their houses: for example, Venus is in her proper face when making a sextile aspect to either luminary, provided she be occidental to the Sun, but oriental to the Moon, agreeably to the primary arrangement of her houses." (Ashmand, 37-38) In R. Schmidt's translation of this section we find the following in a footnote: ". . . even though the term 'face' is generally synonymous with 'affiliation' in the pre-Ptolemaic tradition, it also has the deviant usage that follows. Decanic face as a dignity is conspicuously absent in Ptolemy's list of dignities, perhaps because of an association which they [the faces, RH.] may have with the extra-zodiacal constellations of the fixed stars, which would be incompatible with Ptolemy's overall tropical approach." (Schmidt trans., *Tetrabiblos Book I*, 46n)

The Arab astrologer Al-Qabisi (Alcabitius) (10th c.), in *The Introduction to Astrology*, page 23 says: "These planets have shares in these signs, some of them by nature, others by accident; those by nature are the house, then the exaltation, then the term, then the triplicity, then the *decan*." (italics mine). On page 29 he lists the decans' rulership in the typical Chaldean order. See Al-Qabisi (Alcabitius), *The Introduction to Astrology, Editions of the Arabic and Latin Texts with an English Translation*, ed. Keiji Yamamoto and Michio Yano Charles Burnett (London: Warburg Institute Publications, 2004).

Al-Biruni (11th c.), in his work differentiates between 'faces' and 'decanates'; faces are ruled in the Chaldean order while the decanates' rulership follows the triplicity sequence. See Al-Biruni, *The Book of Instruction in the Elements of the Art of Astrology*, translated by R. Ramsey Wright (London: Luzac and Co., 1934), 262.

It is clearly evident that Ibn Ezra uses 'face' in its spatial meaning, as an area where a planet has some level of dominion, and not in a sense of some angular phase. In the *The Beginning of Wisdom* on page 23 Ibn Ezra has the following "The first face, according to the Egyptian astrologers and most other gentile astrologers belongs to Mars, the second to the Sun and the third to Jupiter, but according to the Hindu astrologers the first [face] belongs to Mars, the second to the Sun and the third to Venus." In other places he also specifies Persian and Babylonian astrologers as the source, and consistently follows the Chaldean sequence of: Mars, Sun, Venus, Mercury, Moon, Saturn, Jupiter. Elsewhere, Ptolemy's 'phase' is also mentioned by Ibn Ezra as a form of planetary strength, but not given a specific name, nor quoting Ptolemy. Here, he seems to choose the prevalent 'spatial' usage and ignore the 'phase' one. See Avraham Ibn Ezra, *The Beginning of Wisdom*, translated by Meira Epstein (Reston, VA: ARHAT Publications, 1998).

computations. The number of degrees of one of the pivots[1] (of the nativity) ought to be the same as the number of degrees in its sign[2] of the planet with the most dominion. The astrologers that came after him got confused as some say that if the ruler is closer to the tenth house [cusp] than to the rising degree, we shall first assign to the [degree of the] line of the midheaven the number of the ruler's degrees, and from it we can extract the rising degree as explained in the *Book of Tables*; likewise if it is closer to the beginning of the fourth house. But if it is closer to the first pivot (ascendant) or to the similar pivot which is the beginning of the seventh house, then we shall assign to the number of the rising degree the number of the degrees of the ruler. If the [birth of the] native was between the time of the opposition and the time of the conjunction, we shall extract the degree of the opposition[3] with much precision, and we shall seek the ruler of the degree and do [the correction] as written [above].

Those that came after him confused it even more; [5] for some say that we shall always take the degree of the Moon whether it is above or below the earth at the moment of the opposition, and others say that we shall always take the degree of the luminary that is above the earth at the moment of birth.[4] Ptolemy also said that the two luminaries rule over man, and

---

[1] 'Pivot' is originally the translation suggested by Robert Schmidt for the Greek *kentron* (κέντρον) which means 'goad'. It is also the source of the English word 'center'. Schmidt has used it in all of his translations from Greek, and the Hebrew word translated here means much the same thing as *kentron*. It is used in two ways: 1) to refer to the actual degrees of the Ascendant, Midheaven, Descendant, and *Imum Coeli*; 2) or to refer to the first, tenth, seventh, and fourth houses which were by Ibn Ezra's time defined by the Ascendant, Midheaven, Descendant and *Imum Coeli* respectively. [RH]

[2] To summarize: In book III chapter 3, Ptolemy explains the necessity for this procedure due to the imprecision of the measuring devices of his time. The steps are: First find the ascendant as approximated by the device that is used. Then, determine the planet that has most dominion in the place of the lunation prior to birth. Then, determine the numerical value of its degree in the sign where that planet was found at the time of birth (i.e. natal position). Make that numerical value the number of degree rising in the sign that was first found to be nearest the ascendant.

[3] This is the case when a Full Moon preceded the birth of the native.

[4] It is the day or night factor and the phase of the Moon that determines the choice. Also, it is interesting that Ptolemy does not say what to do when both luminaries are above the horizon in a preventional birth, i.e., one that occurs after a full moon (opposition) and before the new. [RH]

therefore this is found (applies) only in the nativity of a person and not in the nativity of animals and birds.[1] Others said that we should always take the number of one of the pivots according to the number of the degree of the ruler, and we shall do it thus: We should always look to see which one is close[er] to the moment of birth and according to its number we shall assign to [the number of degrees of] one of the pivots the number of degrees of that ruler.

These are the equations that the practitioners of the judgments of the signs relied on, and they are false equations as I have tried them many times with a perfect astrolabe, reckoned the exact moment of birth, and have not found the degree of one of the pivots [to be the same] as the number of the degrees of the ruler (of the prenatal lunation). Then I thought the error might be in the determination of the ruler; so I reckoned the [place of the] rest of the planets and I did not find [among] the luminaries nor the planets [one] whose degree is like that of one of the pivots, except when there is an error in the time of birth of more than one third of an hour. Therefore, it became clear to me that these equations are nonsense. A Hindu astrologer mentioned three other equations, and they are all useless. The truth is [to be found in] the equations of Enoch, except that they need two corrections, for I have tried them in this way many times.

THE EQUATIONS OF ENOCH[2]

[Rectification – The Trutine of Hermes]

Enoch[3] said that invariably in the nativity of a person the place of the

---

[1] The passage "and therefore this is found only in the nativity of a person and not in the nativity of animals and birds," is omitted in the Latin versions. [RH]

[2] The following method is usually referred to as the Trutine or Trutina of Hermes. It is mentioned in most pre-modern astrological writings on nativities. [RH]

[3] In the Latin version of the text "Hermes" appears wherever the Hebrew has "Enoch." It was believed by many medievals that Hermes and Enoch were the same person. [RH]. [Additional by MBE] Enoch (חֲנוֹךְ) is a legendary-mythological figure, seventh generation from Adam, who is very briefly mentioned in the Bible and the Talmud, but fully described in the Apocryphal literature. Like Hermes Trismegistus, he has access to divine knowledge which

Moon at the moment of birth is the rising degree at the moment of the dripping [of the seed] in the womb,[1] and the rising degree at the moment of birth that [degree] is the place where the Moon was at the moment of the dripping in the womb. Therefore, if we know [6] the moment of the dripping, we could know the moment of birth, and if we know the moment of birth, we could know when the moment of the dripping was.

We shall do it thus. We shall look at the moment of birth [to see] whether the Moon was below the earth or above it; if we find her in the rising degree, we would know that the native stayed in his mother's belly [the length of] the mean period, which is 273 days. If the Moon was in the setting degree, then its period [was] the short period, which is 259 days. And if it was below the earth even [as much as] one degree close to the setting degree, then its period was the long period which is 287 days.

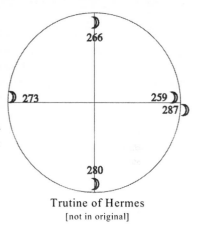

Trutine of Hermes
[not in original]

There are seven days between the [periods corresponding to the] pivots. Therefore, if the Moon was at the beginning of the line of the mid-heaven, then the period was 266 [days], and if she was at the beginning of the line of the [lower] pivot, then the period [was] 280 days.

If the Moon was not at the beginning of one of the pivots, we shall take the distance of her place from the beginning of the pivot that [she just] passed, and we shall take for every thirteen degrees one day, and whatever the total of days, we shall add them to the number that would be proper for the period if the Moon had been at the beginning of [that] pivot. If there is a remainder of the degrees that does not divide by thirteen,

he writes down and brings back to earth.

[1] In other medieval works it is clear that the relevant moment was the moment of the father's ejaculation not the moment of the conception which is technically the joining of the sperm and the egg. The notion that the trutine finds the moment of conception in the modern technical sense is modern. Also, the Latin has a word that means 'draining' or 'dripping' *guttatio*. [RH]

[then] look [to see] if the [remaining] degrees are seven (or more) [and] take one day, and if less [than seven], ignore them.[1]

Then you look at the day of the dripping, and this is how you reckon the hours [for the] rising degree at the moment of the dripping to be the place of the Moon at the moment of birth. This number that you have [found] is an approximation, since at times you will [have to] add hours or subtract according to the distance of the hours of the dripping from the hours of birth.[2] [7]

The astrologers who came after Enoch concurred with him about these equations, and I have also tried [it] and succeeded, except that there are times when it requires one of two corrections.

Everything we said [above] is true for those born close to nine months [of pregnancy], which is most people. But there are times when the child is born in the seventh month and also in the eleventh month, and therefore I will mention to you the corrections.

Look [to see] if the time is close to the [computed date[3] for the] birth, and [see whether] Venus or Mercury, which are the inferior planets and whose nature is close to that of the Moon, enter the place where the Moon is supposed to be at the moment of birth, and [whether] Venus or Mercury have dominion in that place. Then look [for] the moment when the Moon is in quartile aspect with the planet found in the [afore]mentioned degree. [If so,] then the child will come out seven days earlier than the proper period, [and that is] because Venus and Mercury are swift [and therefore] they [can] act like the Moon, unlike the rest of the planets. If Venus or Mercury are found in that degree but have no rulership in the degree, even if the Moon aspects it by quartile, the child will not come out until the Moon reaches the degree at the completion of the allotted term.

---

[1] In other words, round off the number of degrees divided by 13. [RH]

[2] The Latin text has the following: *deinde respice diem guttationis: et adequa horas taliter ut sit gradus ascendens in hora guttationis gradus lune: nati hora: et numerus tibi completus est modo propinquo. Aliquando enim addes horas: aut subtrahes secundum distantiam horarum a puncto guttationis a puncto nati.* [Punctuation as in the original] "Then look at the day of the dropping [of the seed]: and adjust the time in such a way so that the ascending degree at the time of the dropping [of the seed] is the degree of the Moon at the time of birth. Sometimes you will add time or [sometimes] you will subtract according to the distance from the [ascending] point of the dropping [of the seed and] from the point [of the Moon] of the birth." These last two points should be identical.

[3] According to the rules described above.

The second correction: Look [to see] if Mars enters the place of the Moon at the moment of the dripping and Mars is in its domicile or its exaltation and the time is close to seven days from the end of the term and the Moon has joined Mars. [If so,] then the child will come out before the term.

[The Months of Pregnancy]

Astrologers have said that Saturn rules the first month of the (gestation) term since the seed needs [some]one that will steady it and form it. Jupiter rules the second month for it indicates the vegetative soul. Mars rules the third month and then the fetus moves. The Sun rules the fourth month and then the spirit of life enters it. Venus rules the fifth month and it shapes all the limbs and beautifies the whole form. [8] Mercury rules the sixth month and it differentiates all the organs and completes their shaping. The Moon rules the seventh month and she will strengthen each organ, so if the child comes out in this month, it shall live because the Moon governs life. Then Saturn returns to be the ruler of the eighth month and the movement of the fetus slows down.[1] So, if there are circumstances, whether in the body of the woman because of a difficult illness that happens to her or because of the mind such as sudden fear and worry, and the fetus comes out in that month, [both] it and its mother will die. Jupiter rules the ninth month and that is why most newborns come out in this month. [If] it delays until the tenth month, which is ruled by Mars, it will also come out of the belly because Mars' nature indicates a lot of movement, except that those born in its month will live [only a] little [time]. The one born in the eleventh month, which is ruled by the Sun, will live more [time].

And now I shall begin to mention all the matters of the native, the matters of his parents, his siblings, and his wife according to the ancients. Ptolemy said that even though the rising degree at the moment of the dripping ought to be the principal [horoscope], the rising degree at the moment of birth participates with it. Enoch said that from the rising degree at the moment of the dripping we could know all the things that would happen to the fetus until it comes out of its mother's belly, and from the rising degree at the moment of birth we could know all the things that will happen to him in the world in [accordance with] the place where it came

---

[1] The Latin has *minuetur*, 'is diminished.' [RH]

out, because as it comes out it receives the influence of the air (ambient), and from that influence it receives the influence of the higher spirit according to the co-mixture of his body and the nature of the ambient, and [Enoch] spoke correctly.[1]

Therefore we have no need for the rising degree at the moment of the dripping, and in order to make it easier for the students I have followed [9] the [other] astrologers in explaining the matters of nativities according to the twelve houses.

THE FIRST HOUSE

[Temperament]

The first house indicates the soul, the mind, intelligence, faith, the body and the life of the person. Ptolemy said that we should combine the nature of the rising sign with the nature of the time [in which] the native is born. For if the season is hot because it is in the summer time and the native is born in the second quadrant which is from midday until night,[2] then this

---

[1] Ptolemy also says that in the *Tetrabiblos*, book III, chapter II: ". . . the origin by conception affords the inference of occurrences which take effect previously to the birth, whereas the origin by birth can, of course, be available only for such as arise subsequently." (Ashmand, 72)

Ptolemy's systematic doctrine can be summarized as follows: The moment of conception is the primary creative cause, whereby the seed receives the influence of the prevailing ambient. In subsequent periods it will be imbued only with qualities that are proper for those impressed on it by that primary cause. The origin by birth is a secondary beginning, yet in no respect deficient. It is equal to the conception in its efficacy and is much more complete even though later in time. Conception is the mere generation of the human seed while at birth the infant acquires qualities which it could not possess in the womb, and are proper to human nature alone such as the action of the senses and the movement of body and limbs. ". . . nature, after completing the formation in the womb, always effects the birth in immediate obedience to some certain positions of the Ambient, corresponding and sympathising with the primary position which operated the incipient formation." (Ashmand, ibid.) In other words – the birth chart maintains continuity with the conception chart and preserves its primary properties. The moment of conception is of supreme importance, but when it cannot be ascertained, the moment of birth can be just as efficient in assessing future developments.

[2] Sun between the Midheaven and the Descendant.

indicates that the nature of the native is very hot [relative to] the region one is born in. It is the same judgment for the cold season when the rising sign is of the cold [signs] and the native is born at night, and it is the same judgment for the wet and the dry seasons.

Enoch said that we should always look to the nature of the rising sign and to the nature of its lord; if it aspects the rising degree in one of the aspects, or [if] the exaltation ruler or the bound ruler or the triplicity ruler or the face ruler [are aspecting], we shall co-mix the nature of the [rising] sign with the nature of the aspecting ruler. If there is a planet[1] in the rising sign, we will co-mix its nature with the nature of the ruler. In the same way we will look to the planet the Moon is [joined] with, and the sign where she is, as well as the bound and the [other planets] aspecting her, and her position with respect to the Sun.

Ptolemy said that we should co-mix with the rising sign the [co-]rising figure in the east from among the thirty-six forms that are outside the wheel [of the zodiac],[2] and I say that we have no need for those forms for they are far from the inhabited region and also very high and very far.[3] And the truth is [in] Enoch's words.

[The Ruler of the Nativity]

Ptolemy and Doroneus[4] said that we should always seek the planet that rules the nativity, and this is how we shall find it. We know that the places of [the] life[-givers] are five: the [first] two are the places of the two lights by day and by night; the third is the place of the conjunction of the lights or their oppositions whichever is first [immediately] before the birth of the native; the fourth is the rising degree [10] and the fifth is the Lot of Fortune as I have explained it in *The Book of Reasons for The Beginning of Wisdom*.[5] We will reckon for the ruler of the domicile 5 fortitudes, for the ruler by exaltation 4, for the triplicity ruler 3, for the ruler of the bound

---

[1] A planet other than the ruler.

[2] See *The Beginning of Wisdom*, chapter 2.

[3] Far from the ecliptic, north or south.

[4] The Arabic name for Dorotheus of Sidon.

[5] The text actually reads as: "In *The Book of Reasons for the Beginning of Wisdom*." Ibn Ezra wrote *The Book of Reasons* as commentary and supplement for *The Beginning of Wisdom*. Ibn Ezra himself says in the first sentence of *The Book of Reasons*, "I am hereby laying the foundation for the book *The Beginning of Wisdom*." The Lot of Fortune is mentioned in both books.

2 and for the ruler of the face 1. We will do so for every one that has rulership in all the five places.[1]

We will also look to see if it is [one] of the superior planets and moving away from the Sun and it is in its greatest power; [if so] we will give it [additional] 3 fortitudes, and if in its middle [power], 2 [fortitudes] and if in its minor [power], 1 [fortitude].[2]

We will also look [to evaluate the ruler] with regard to the houses; for the one found in the first house has 12 fortitudes, in the tenth house 11 [fortitudes], in the seventh 10 [fortitudes], in the fourth 9 [fortitudes], in the eleventh 8 [fortitudes], in the fifth 7 [fortitudes], in the second 6 [fortitudes], in the eighth 5 [fortitudes], in the ninth 4 [fortitudes], in the third 3 [fortitudes], in the twelfth 2 [fortitudes] and in the sixth 1 [fortitude], and according to the nature of the ruler so is the nature of the native's body.

[Physical Appearance]

If this ruler is on the wheel of the ecliptic,[3] the native will be thin; if it has latitude, he will be fat, and according to its latitude so you will judge. If its latitude is southern, his movements will be nimble, and if northern,

---

[1] The places of Prorogation as Ptolemy calls them, are the 1st house, the 10th, 11th, 7th, and 9th houses. The chart factors that can operate as life givers, or Prorogators, are the Sun, Moon, New or Full Moon before birth, Ascendant, or Lot of Fortune. In the text we find the phrase 'places of life' occasionally used for both Prorogators and Places of Prorogation. It seems that the author is relying on the context and the prior knowledge of his reader.

[2] This refers to the superior planets, Mars, Jupiter and Saturn in their oriental position in relation with the faster moving Sun as it separates from them following a conjunction. In *The Beginning of Wisdom*, chapter five, and with much detail in chapter six, Ibn Ezra lists this phase as an additional strength a planet might have, from the dexter sextile aspect until its first station when it becomes retrograde. The sinister aspects with the Sun are not as strong since the planet is approaching the conjunction with the Sun which will render it powerless – combust. Here, in this scoring system, these phases also confer points. [Additional by RH] The preceding sentence is completely omitted from the two Latin editions of this text that I have seen. This might be important or it may be that the Hebrew is from a variant textual tradition.

[3] The ecliptic is consistently called by Ibn Ezra: '*heshev afudat hagalgal'* (חשב אפודת הגלגל), which can be translated as 'the computation of the engirdling wheel'. Henceforth, 'the wheel of the ecliptic' will be used.

[they will be] heavy. If the rising [sign] is of the signs that are long in ascension, especially if the rising degree is in the first face [of the sign] and the Moon is [also] in a sign of long ascension, then we shall judge that the native will be taller than his parents, and the opposite [is true] if it is in the ones of short ascension.

In the same way you will judge regarding the native's beauty relative to his parents. Know that the signs that are of human form, as we have explained in the book *The Beginning of Wisdom*, will indicate beauty if the rising sign is in one of them, [or] the ruler and the Moon are in one of them, especially if Venus aspects the rising [degree], the Moon, or the [nativity] ruler; then [the native] will be handsome and good looking. The signs that indicate medium beauty are Scorpio, Capricorn, and Pisces. Zahel Ben Basar the Jew said that the ruler of the face [in the sign] indicates the face of the person; and [he] said [11] that he tried it many times. And he is right when the ruler of the face aspects the rising degree. I have already explained in the book *The Beginning of Wisdom* the nature of every sign and all that it indicates [for] one who is born in [each] one of the faces.

Now I shall mention to you whether the infant will be reared,[1] and you should heed to make no judgment except by two proper witnesses (testimonies),[2] and now I shall explain to you the testimonies, their admissibility and their rejection.

THE TESTIMONIES

The testimony of any planet that is burnt in the light of the Sun is rejected

---

[1] This topic is discussed further below and is usually one of the traditional schemes for the ages of life and the planets that rule them. Within the context of health and the length of life it actually attempts to determine whether the newborn will survive infancy and grow to adulthood.

[2] The Hebrew phrase *'shnei edim ksherim'* (שני עדים כשרים) is a term used in Talmudic discussions of legal ruling stating that evidence can be accepted only when there are at least "two kosher witnesses," meaning 'reliable qualified witnesses'. The context here indicates that the testimonies consist not only of aspects but of other conditions as well.

15

for a good [outcome] and for a bad one it stands.[1]

The testimony of any retrograde planet, [whether] for good or bad [outcome,] is rejected.

The testimony of any planet that is in a cadent house is rejected except for the ninth house; for if it is [found] there, it is half a testimony, and if the Sun is there, it is a complete testimony.[2]

The testimony of a planet [found] in one of the pivots, for a good or bad [outcome], is complete.

The testimony of a planet [found] in one of the three adjacent houses[3] is half a testimony, and if Jupiter is in the eleventh house, or Venus is in the fifth [house], then it is a complete testimony.[4]

The one [found] in the eighth house, if for a good [outcome], its testimony is rejected, [and] if for a bad [outcome], its testimony stands.

If the Moon is in a [bodily] conjunction[5] with a benefic planet, it is a true testimony for a good [outcome], and if in aspect with a benefic planet, it is half a good testimony, and if [it is] in a [bodily] conjunction with the harmful planets, it is a complete testimony for a bad [outcome].

If the Moon is under the earth at the moment of birth and she confers her power to a planet under the earth, it is a complete testimony for ill [regardless] whether the planet is benefic or malefic, and it is the same when the Moon is above the earth conferring her power to a planet under the earth.

If the Moon is above the earth and she confers her power to a planet above the earth, it is a complete testimony for good, and it is the same when the Moon is under the earth conferring her power to a planet above the earth if it is one of the benefics, and that is like two valid testimonies unless the planet is combust or retrograde, for then the testimony is dismissed.

If it is one of the malefics and it receives the Moon favorably, it is a complete testimony for good [results], and if [the malefic planet does] not

---

[1] A combust planet cannot produce good results, but there might be times when a negative result is the desired outcome.

[2] The 9th house is the Joy of the Sun.

[3] Adjacent to the Angles: The 2nd, 5th and 11th houses. The 8th house, although adjacent to the 7th, is an evil place.

[4] The 11th and the 5th houses are the Joys of Jupiter and Venus respectively.

[5] The word is *be'makhberet* (במחברת) meaning 'joined together', 'conjoined' which later astrology calls 'conjunction'. Further down 'in aspect' is *bemabat* (במבט).

[receive it favorably], then the testimony is dismissed. And if the Moon is above [12] the earth conferring her power to a planet above the earth, whether it is a benefic or a malefic planet, it is a complete testimony for a good [outcome].

[When] the Moon confers her power to the lord of the eighth house and it is a benefic, this is half a testimony for adversity, and if it is a malefic, it is a complete testimony [for adversity]. In the same way as you have observed the Moon you will look at the ruler [of the chart], for it is the principal [one].[1]

[The Years of Rearing]

Ptolemy said that the period of the rearing is a whole year until the Sun returns to its place at the time of birth. The ancients said that the period of rearing is four years, until the native passes the four elements (natures), and in each one of these years the matters of the native will be according to the nature of the planets and their aspects in these four signs – the first, the second, the third and the fourth – and according to the influence of the rulers of these four [signs] and according to the change of their place in each annual revolution,[2] as I shall explain in the [chapter on the] revolutions.

Al Andruzaqar bin Zari Fariq said that the first ruler of the triplicity in the rising sign will indicate the first one-third of the rearing years, the second

---

[1] The Latin has *Et sicut respicis lunam ita principantem aspice. hec est radix.* "And just as you look at the Moon, look at the ruling planet in the same way, for this planet is a foundational planet." [RH]

[2] The sequence is not clear – possibly by Profection of the Ascendant. [Additional by RH] The Latin has: *Antiqui autem dixerunt annos nutritionis .4. esse quousque .4. nature super natum per transierint: et quod quodlibet annorum istorum est maneries nati: secundum naturam stellarum: et aspectum earum in locis .4. primum .2ᵐ. 3ᵐ. ac .4ᵐ. Et secundum fortitudinem principaliorem in hiis .4. Et secundum mutationem loci eius in cuiuslibet anni revolutione: . . .* "Moreover, the ancients said that the years of rearing are four until the four [elements] of nature have passed over the native and that each of these years is a manner [of being] for the native according to the nature of the stars and their aspects in the four places, the first, the second, the third, and the fourth; and according to the strength of the planet which has the most rulership in these four [places], and according to the change of its place in the revolution of each year." [RH]

ruler of the triplicity will indicate the middle one-third of the rearing years, and the last [ruler will indicate] the last [one-third of the rearing years.]

[Character and Personality]

Now I shall begin to speak of the soul of the native. Ptolemy said that we should always look to the place of Mercury and the ruler of its place, and the place of the Moon, and according to the nature of the ruler so will be his soul.[1] He also said that if the ruler is in a changeable[2] sign, the native will be inconstant; if in a fixed sign, the native will keep his word; and if in a bi corporeal sign, his nature will alternate this way one time and another way at another time.

If the ruler is one of the superiors and it is oriental of the Sun in its greatest strength,[3] then he will have an elevated soul, brave and strong, full of [13] wisdom and intelligence, and if the superior planet is occidental [of the Sun,[4]] this will be an inferior soul doing all its actions in deception; and if the ruler is combust, all his life he will be in fear, worry and anger.

If the ruler is one of the inferior planets and it is occidental, according to its strength (or influence) in the west so will be the soul of the native. Ptolemy said that if the Moon is configured with Mercury by aspect or conjunction, and both are aspecting the rising degree, then the soul of the person is whole and his mind will overcome his desire; he will not do anything except in honesty and judgment, and he will not lose his mental faculties even in sickness. If it is the opposite (Moon not properly configured with Mercury), then all his dealings will be in disorder, especially when sick.

Indian astrologers said that if the planet of intelligence, Mercury, is in an opposition or a quartile aspect with Saturn, then it indicates a wise

---

[1] The following description is of what we would call character, personality and the mind.

[2] The cardinals signs (Aries, Cancer, Libra and Capricorn) are traditionally called Movable or Changeable, demarcating the change of the seasons.

[3] Mars, Jupiter, or Saturn, in their opening phase from the Sun (rising before the Sun), before their first station.

[4] Rising or setting after the Sun. In this phase the superior planet is heading towards a conjunction with the Sun – first 'under the beams' and then into combustion conditions, i.e. becoming invisible.

soul that produces sciences and intelligences, especially if one of them is the ruler. They also said that they have found that if Mercury is in one of Saturn's domiciles, then it indicates depth of thought and knowledge of secrets and hidden things, especially if Mercury is the ruler.

Ptolemy said in the *Book of Fruit*[1] that as is the influence of Saturn in the nativity and its dominion over it, such will be patience and hard work found in him (the person); as is the influence of Jupiter such will be the strength of the vegetative soul that makes the body grow; as is the influence of Mars so will be [the expression of] his anger; as is the influence of the Sun so will be his thoughts and morality; as is the influence of Venus so will be his desires; as is the influence of Mercury so will be his wisdom and intelligence; and as is the influence of the Moon so will be the habits of his body.

He also said that if Saturn aspects the Moon, all his life he will be with many worries and [troubled] thoughts; if Jupiter [aspects the Moon], he will rejoice with love of justice and peace; if Mars [aspects the Moon], he will be in anger and rage day and night; if the Sun [aspects the Moon], he will seek authority; if Venus [aspects the Moon], he will seek food and drink and sexual intercourse; and if Mercury [aspects the Moon], he will seek all kinds of learning. [14]

If no planet aspects the Moon, the person will be slow in all his dealings, and if the aspecting [planets] are many, each one of them will confer its nature according to its influence. I have already mentioned the influences of all the planets in the book *The Beginning of Wisdom*.

[The Measure of Life – by the Years of the Planets]

Now I shall speak of the [length of] life of the native. Always observe the place of the Sun if the native was born by day. For if it is in the tenth house or the eleventh as reckoned according to the latitude of the place,[2] [regardless of] whether the sign [of the Sun] is masculine or feminine, and if one of the rulers of its place is beholding it by any aspect, then we could know the number of years of life from the place of the Sun when we direct

---

[1] There is no such reference in the *Centiloquy* even though that is the book to which Ibn Ezra seems to be referring. [RH]

[2] This qualification of the houses echoes the discussion about equal house, or whole-sign house systems versus mundane house systems, and it also pertains to the definition of aspects. See Ashmand, 91-96.

its degree, as I shall explain. If the Sun is in one of the [afore]mentioned places and none of the rulers of its place is aspecting it, we shall seek the measure of life from another place. [We shall do] the same if it (the Sun) is in the seventh house, or in the ninth house which is its house of joy, and the sign is masculine;[1] [then] we shall seek the measure of life from the ruler if it is aspecting [the Sun].

If there is no ruler aspecting [the Sun] there, we shall seek the measure of life from the Moon.[2] If we find her in the first or the seventh house, [regardless of] whether the signs are masculine or feminine, or in the tenth or the eleventh house, and the signs are feminine, and one of the rulers of her place is aspecting her, we shall take the measure of life from that ruler; but if no ruler is aspecting [her] there, we shall leave it.

This is the opinion of Enoch, the Ancients, and Ptolemy, except that there is a disagreement between them and Ptolemy for they say that if the Moon is in the third house, which is her house of joy, or in the fourth or fifth house, and the signs are feminine, and there is a ruler [of that place] aspecting her, we shall take the measure of life from it (the ruler), and

---

[1] The tenth and eleventh houses are in the quadrant that is defined as masculine, which is appropriate for the Sun and therefore does not require further qualifications. The ninth and the seventh houses are in a feminine quadrant, and therefore require the sign to be masculine, in order to strengthen the Sun against the disharmony of gender. The reverse logic applies to the Moon, which follows immediately in the text.

[2] [Additional by RH] Here is what the Latin says: *Quod si fuerit in locis predictis: sed nullus principantium in eius loco eum aspiciat querenda est tunc vita ab alio loco. Et similiter si fuerit in .9°. aut .7. hoc enim est locus sui gaudii. Si signum fuerit masculinum querenda est vita principaliori si aspiciat. Quod si nullus principalium existit aspiciens querenda est vita a loco lune quam si invenerimus in domo prima. aut in .7. si fuerit masculinum signum aut femininum. Aut in .10°. vel .11°. dum tamen sint signa feminina et aliquis principantium in suo loco: ipsam aspiciat: accipienda est vita a principante.* . . "But if he [the Sun] is in the aforesaid places but none of the planets ruling in his place aspect him, one must then seek life from another place. And likewise if the Sun is in the 9th or 7th (for the 9th is the house of his joy), if the sign is masculine, one must seek life from the ruler if he aspects the Sun. But if none of the rulers is aspecting, one must seek life from the place of the Moon; if we find her in the first house, or in the 7th whether the sign is masculine or feminine, or in the 10th or 11th houses, provided that they are feminine signs, and one of the planets which rules in her place aspects her, one must take [the indication of] life from the planet which rules [the place of the Moon]." [RH]

Ptolemy says that we should never take the measure of life from a planet that is under the earth,[1] and my opinion is inclined [to agree] with him for I have tried it. The same [was] also said [by] Doroneus, who is the chief of the judges (astrologers).

If the luminaries are not [found] in the [afore]mentioned places, or they are there and there is no ruler [15] aspecting [them], we shall look to see if the nativity was after the conjunction of the luminaries. We shall look to see if the place of the conjunction is in the first pivot,[2] the setting one (seventh house), the culminating one (tenth house), or the house adjacent to it which is the eleventh house, and [whether] there is a ruler [of that place] aspecting [it]; [then] we shall take the measure of life from it. [But] if the conjunction was not in the [afore]mentioned places, or it was there and there was no ruler aspecting, we shall seek the measure of life from the rising degree. If we find a ruler [of this degree] aspecting [it], we shall take the measure of life from it; but if there is no ruler aspecting [it], we shall direct from the rising degree to an abscission place, as I shall explain. Every native who[se chart] is like this his years will be few.[3]

If the nativity was after the opposition of the luminaries, we shall look to see when the moment of the opposition took place and we shall know which of the luminaries was above the earth. We shall observe whether that luminary was in one of the places that I have mentioned for the conjunction, and [whether] there is a ruler aspecting [it], [and] we shall take the measure of life from the ruler.

If the luminary was not in one of the [afore]mentioned places, or it was there but there is no ruler aspecting [it], we shall look to see in which place the Lot of Fortune is. If we find it in one of the places I mentioned

---

[1] *Tetrabiblos,* Ashmand, 89..

[2] Of the nativity. On the use of 'pivot' see page 7, note 1.

[3] This is not a Ptolemaic doctrine but it is found in Hellenistic sources as well as Arabic and medieval Latin ones. That a ruler must aspect a hyleg is found as early Dorotheus of Sidon (1st century C.E.), Valens *Anthology* (2nd century C.E.), and Paulus Alexandrinus (4th century C.E.). See Dorotheus of Sidon, *Carmen Astrologicum,* ed. David Pingree (Leipzig: Teubner, 1976), 242-245; Vettius Valens, *The Anthology, Book II (Concl.), & Book III,* translated by Robert Schmidt (Berkeley Springs, WV: Golden Hind Press, 1994), 27-33; and Dorian Greenbaum, trans., *Late Classical Astrology: Paulus Alexandrinus and Olympiodorus* (Reston, VA: ARHAT Publications, 2001), 75. The earliest connection that I am aware between this condition and a short life expectancy is to be found in Omar of Tiberias. Omar of Tiberias, *Three Books on Nativities,* translated by Robert Hand (Berkeley Springs, WV: Golden Hind Press, 1997), 4-5).[RH]

for the conjunction and there is a ruler aspecting [it], we shall take the measure of life from it. If it is [not] in one of these places, or it is there and there is no ruler aspecting, then we shall seek the measure of life from the rising degree.

If the native was [born] at night, we shall [first] seek the measure of life from the Moon in the way we mentioned [before]. [If the Moon cannot be taken], then we shall seek the place of the Sun. If it is in the first house and there is a ruler aspecting [it], we shall take the measure of life from the ruler, but if the Sun is there and there is no ruler aspecting [it], we shall look to see if the native was [born] after the conjunction or the opposition [of the luminaries] and do as I have shown you without adding or subtracting [a thing]. Doroneus said [that] you should look to the ruler of the[se] five places of life and from it you could know the measure of life, and he spoke properly.[1] [16]

Ptolemy [said that] if we find the ruler (of life) in the first house, the tenth, the seventh, or the eleventh,[2] [then] we shall take the measure of life from it, but those that came after him did not agree, and they are right. The Persians call the five places of life Hillaj and they call[3] the ruler Alchocoda. The meaning of these words are male and female; the reason is [that they are] like a father and a mother sought for the native in the wheel.[4]

Now you should look to the ruler (the Alchocoda), [and] if it is [one]

---

[1] Dorotheus, ibid. [RH]

[2] That is, only the houses above the earth, excluding the 8th, the 9th and the 12th.

[3] The Hebrew word is *'ve'he'linu'* (והליגו), which usually means 'blamed, accused, alleged' or 'complained', but makes sense here as 'called'.

[4] The Latin has the following for this passage: *Et perse nominaverunt .5. loca vite: yleg. et principantem alcochodren. quorum nominum ex primo masculum est et femininum, id est pater et mater. Que in nato querere debes in circulo.* "And the Persians have designated these fives places Hyleg, and the ruler, the Alcochodren. The words for these [are] in the first instance masculine, and [the second] feminine, that is, father and mother. In a birth you should seek these out in the circle." The Latin *Alcochodren* is of course equivalent to Ibn Ezra's *Alchocoda*. There are many spellings and transliterations of the original word which is *kadkhudah*, the 'al' prefix simply meaning 'the'. Where the *hillaj* (most commonly *hyleg* in Latin astrology) gives an indication concerning the vitality of the native, the *Alchocoda* indicates the number of years of a native's life. It must be one of the rulers of the *Hillaj*, and also make an aspect to it. [RH]

of the superior planets, oriental,[1] direct in its motion, or at the beginning of the second station at [about] forty-five degrees[2] and it is in one of the pivots, or if the ruler is Jupiter and it is in the eleventh house,[3] [then] the native will live according to the great number of years of the planet; and if it is in one of the adjacent houses, his life will be according to mean years [of the planet]; and if it is in one of the cadent houses, his life will be according to its minor years.

Be cautious; [for] if you find the ruler, whether a superior or inferior planet, under the light of the Sun, you should not observe it but seek another ruler. If the ruler is retrograde, observe how many years [of life] it indicates and find out how many days it has been retrograde; and according to their proportion to the [total number of] days from the first station to the second station that much you will take out of two fifths[4] of the years of the planet; and that result you will subtract from the years of the planet and this will be the number of years of [the native's] life. If the method of proportion is difficult for you, multiply 2/5 of the planet's years by the number of days of its retrograde motion and divide the result by the number [of days] between the two stations; the result is the number you have to subtract.

If the ruler is one of the inferiors, look to see if it is occidental or oriental until its computed degree is nine signs,[5] and it is in one of the

---

[1] Rising before the Sun.

[2] The Latin has *super .45. gradus.* "above 45 degrees." [RH]. [Additional by MBE] The word is '*al'* (על) which, depending on the idea expressed, could mean 'on, over, at, about,' and in a mathematical context even 'by' as in 'multiply by'. If we add the letter 'מ' ('*mem*') as in 'מעל' ('*me'al* '), it changes the meaning to 'over, above'. Yet, this is a speculation on my part, since the Hebrew lettering in the manuscript does not suggest that.

[3] The joy of Jupiter. [RH]

[4] The text clearly says 'two fifths' , which appears to be used as a constant applied to the years of the planet, to which the proportion of the retrograde period is applied.

[5] The phrase 'until its computed degree is nine signs' presents an unresolved question: It seems to refer to a measure of some kind of an orb. Planetary orbs are usually measured in degrees, not in signs. Moreover, it is unclear as to the reference points of these nine signs. Orientality is mentioned but the inferior planets, Mercury and Venus, whether oriental or occidental, can never be more than one or two signs, respectively, away from the Sun. The studied manuscripts consistently use this phrase and do not offer a helpful variation. The Latin translation is does not offer any clue either: [Additional by RH] The Latin has

pivots, or the adjacent [houses], or the cadent [ones; and] do (proceed) in the manner of the superior [planets]. If it is one of the superior [planets], [17] occidental, [and therefore] weak, or one of the inferior [planets] oriental, [and therefore] weak, it cannot grant its greater years even when it is in a pivot.

[When] a benefic planet aspects the ruler from one of the pivots, or [from] the [houses] adjacent to the culminating pivot, or to the lower heaven [pivot], then it will add the number of its lesser years regardless whether its aspect is of harmony or hostility. If one of the malefics beholds the ruler [by] a quartile or an opposition aspect and the malefic is in one of the pivots or the two adjacent ones, it will subtract [years of life] according to its lesser years. Doroneus said that the addition or subtraction [of years] is only according to the number of degrees of the distance of the aspect from its completion (the orb). The learned man called Al Bazidag brought in his book [some] tables, which he called Titles,[1] to know the measure of life from. These are fit to be burned in fire furnaces for there is no validity in them.

[The Measure of Life – by Directions]

Now I shall tell you a true and tried thing. Know that all that I have mentioned to you is close to the truth, for when we know the measure of life, we shall direct the place of life that is proper for directing. So if at such a time it arrives at a place that cuts off [life],[2] the native will die that year. If it does not arrive there but in a few more years, the native will not die until the place of life arrives at the place of abscission, except that in those years that are added to the number of the years of the ruler he will live [through] them [afflicted] with many illnesses. If the place of life arrives at a place of abscission before the completion of the number of years of the ruler, and the year (the age) is close to the years of the ruler,

---

donec fuerit eius pars equata .9. signis . . . "until its degree (*pars*) has been equated 9 signs, and . . ." [RH]

   [1] This name looks is unfamiliar to me. [Addition by RH] The Latin has *sortes* which means "lots."

   [2] Abscission place. Also called Anaretic place in the *Tetrabiblos*. Abscission place.

[he] will die that year.[1]

Know [that] if the places of life are proper for taking the measure of life when they are in the places that I have mentioned, and the[ir] aspecting rulers are many, the native will live many years, and one abscission place cannot cut off his life, until two or three of the abscission [places] will combine, and [then] he will die.

Ptolemy said that if the place of life is in the descending quadrant of the wheel, which is [18] [from] the line of the midheaven to the setting degree, we should always direct it backward (contrary to the order of the signs), but Doroneus said that we should not direct it except according to the rule (forward).[2] In the same manner Ptolemy said that the Lot of Fortune should be directed backward, and those who came after him directed both the Lot [of Fortune] and the place of life (Hillaj or Hyleg) when it is in the descending semicircle [both] according to Ptolemy's way and Doroneus' way, and would not issue a final judgment when a place of life reaches an abscission place in one way until it [also] reaches an abscission place in the second way; and in this manner I tried [all] these. The proper directions are as I mentioned in the *Book of Reasons*.

[The Places of Abscission – Cutting Off Life]

These are the places to be feared as cutting off [life], the places of Saturn

---

[1] In the *Tetrabiblos*, Book III (Ashmand, 91-96) Ptolemy details the modes of Prorogation, summarized here: Further considerations involve the quadrant location of the prorogator – succeeding or preceding the midheaven, and its proximity to either the M.C. or the Asc.-Desc.. The dangerous (anaretic) places are the angle of the west (7th house cusp) and aspects to malefic planets. Arrival of the prorogator, by direction, at those places is measured by converting zodiacal rising times (in equatorial degrees) into years. Benefics increase the prorogation, but the malefics diminish it; and Mercury assists the influence of either party with which he may be configured.

[2] [Addition by RH] The Latin has the following: *Et Ptolemeus dicit quod si locus vite fuerit in .4°. circuli recedente: qui est a medio celi ad gradum occidentis. semper in* contrarium *est ducendus. Et doronius dixit nos solum debere ipsum in* rectum *ducere*. "Ptolemy said that if the place of life is in the setting quadrant of the circle, that is, from the midheaven to the setting degree, one must always direct in the *contrary* mode. And Doronius said that we ought only to direct in the *direct* mode." The point here is that contrary and direct are being contrasted so that they are opposed. A possible translation of the Latin would be "backward", and "forward."

and Mars. If the abscissor does not have a distance called latitude from the wheel of the ecliptic, it will cut off [life] for the place of the Sun, the Rising Degree, the Lot of Fortune, the place of the Conjunction of the luminaries or the Opposition (new or full Moon), and [also for the place of] the Moon if she has no latitude from the ecliptic,[1] or if she has the same latitude as that of Saturn or Mars if they are on one side (of the ecliptic).[2] If they are on two [different] sides, they indicate illness but not death, and according to the distance of the latitude between them such will be [the intensity of] the illness for the smaller the distance the more serious the illness will be. Know that if Saturn or Mars have latitude, whether great or small, whether in the northern side or the southern side, they will never cut off life.

You should direct the place of life to the degree that is at the midheaven [together] with Saturn and Mars [Alternative MS: You should direct the place of life and the degree of the midheaven with (to) Saturn and Mars] as explained in *The Book of Tables*.

Know that when Mercury, whether it is oriental or occidental, is in one of the domiciles of the malefics or in aspect with them, its place is also an abscission place, [just] like the place of Saturn and Mars; and if it has latitude, judge it accordingly.

You should know that if Saturn, Mars, or Mercury are under the light of the Sun, they will not cut off life, not even produce illness, for they do not have [19] strength.[3] The opposition aspect of Saturn and of Mars, and

---

[1] A condition when the destroyer is on the ecliptic and is reached by these places, which are also on the ecliptic by definition. The new or full moon are on the ecliptic at the time of a solar or lunar eclipse. The Moon is on the ecliptic when it at the North or South Nodes.

[2] The Hebrew text does not start a new sentence here, but continues with 'or' instead of the 'If', as used here, which presents a variant condition for the Moon. The decision to read the text this way is based on the Latin translation, as well as the inner logic of the procedure of direction which continues right after this one. The places of life – Sun, Asc, and Fortune are by definition on the ecliptic, i.e. have no latitude, whereas the Moon has latitude except when in conjunction with the nodes. The Hebrew for 'or' is אֹ (o) and the word for 'if' is אִם (im). It is plausible to assume a scribal error, due to the similarity of letters, compounded by the absence of punctuation.

[3] Ptolemy has another opinion, in the *Tetrabiblos*, book III, chapter XIV, (Ashmand, 93-94): "It is also to be observed, in all cases, that not any one of such stars [the potential anareta. MBE], whether hostile or auxiliary, is to be left out of the present calculation, on account of its casual position under the sun-beams.

also Mercury, if it is in a bad condition, each of them is an abscission place if it has no latitude, and if it has much latitude, it will produce illness but will not cut off [life]. The quartile aspect from the [above]mentioned [planets] will cut off [life] whether it has latitude or does not have latitude. A trine aspect, dexter or sinister, as well as a sextile aspect, dexter or sinister, will indicate illness but will not cut off [life].[1]

Ptolemy said that if a trine aspect is in signs of short ascension, or a sextile aspect in signs of long ascension according to the latitude of the place, they are both considered as a quartile aspect, and [similarly] if a quartile aspect is in sign[s] of short ascension, it should be considered a sextile aspect,[2] but the astrologers that came after him did not admit that. I have also tried [it] and saw that their words were correct.

When the place of life is the place of the Moon, the rising degree will cut off life when the Moon reaches it by the direction of degrees. The Moon will cut off life at the rising degree but not the other four places of life.[3] The Sun will also cut off [life] at the Moon by conjunction and opposition, but by quartile aspect it will only produce illness and will not cut off [life]. A trine and a sextile aspect will indicate the health of the body. The South Node of the Moon will cut off [life] [when reached by] the Moon. Some of the ancients said that the North Node will also do that but this is not true. The South Node will not cut off [life] with the other places of life. The setting degree is an abscission place for the place of life, and so are the first degree of the pivot of the lower heaven, the Heart of the Scorpion (Antares), the Heart of the Lion (Regulus), the Heart of the Fishes (Fomalhaut), the left Eye of the Bull (Aldebaran), the left shoulder of the Hero (Betelgeuse), the Carrier of the Devil['s Head] (Algol). All these will cut off the places of life if the place of life has latitude on the [same] side of the superior star. If they are on different sides, or the place of life has no latitude, they will produce illness but will

---

This rule must be particularly attended to, because, even though the Moon be not prorogatory, the solar place itself becomes anaretic if shackled by the simultaneous presence of a malefic and not restored to freedom of operation by any benefic.

[1] Again he differs from Ptolemy in the *Tetrabiblos*, book III, chapter XIV: (Ashmand, 92) ". . . in the prorogation made into succeeding signs, the places of the malefics . . . are also sometimes anaretic, by a sextile ray, if in a sign of equal power, obeying or beholding the sign of the prorogator."

[2] *In mundo.*

[3] Sun, Lot of Fortune, New or Full Moon before birth.

not cut off [life]. [20]

Masha'Allah[1] said that the end of a sign will cut off life[2] but that is not true at all, for the division of the wheel is by thought (theoretical) and not in actuality, [and therefore] only if the direction occurs from the sign of a benefic planet, or to the sign of a malefic planet would it produce illness, but it will not cut off [life]. Likewise, when, in directions, the planet leaves a sign where it has dominion [and enters] into a sign where it has no dominion, it will indicate illness but not the cutting off [of life]. It is the same for directions by the bounds when the direction exits the bound of a benefic planet and enters the bound of a malefic one.

Know that a trine or sextile aspect of the Sun, as well as all the aspects of Jupiter and Venus, whether by opposition or a trine or a quartile or a sextile, will always save [from the danger]. There will not be abscission when the place of life reaches the degree of the malefic or its aspect while the aspect is incomplete because of [either] lacking degrees or [having] additional degrees according to the orb of light of the planet, as I have mentioned in the book *The Beginning of Wisdom*.

The conjunction of Jupiter with Venus will save [life]. The conjunction of the Sun is harmful only for the Moon but not for the rest of the places of life. If Jupiter or Venus are under the light of the Sun, they will not bring benefit nor will they save, and likewise, if they are retrograde, or in the sixth house, the twelfth house, or the eighth house.

Know that if Mercury is in the sign of a benefic planet, or in aspect with it, or in its conjunction, it will save [life], as well as its trine and sextile aspect, but its quartile aspect and its opposition will not benefit, nor will it cause harm.

The conjunction of the Moon in all the directions of the places of life saves only [with] the rising degree, as well as by the trine, the sextile, the quartile and the opposition aspect.

Doroneus said that you should always direct the ruler of the nativity, that is, the one that has dominion in all the five places or in most of them, by even (zodiacal) degrees and not by the [ascension] rate of the earth according to any of the placement in the wheel.[3] Many have tried this and

---

[1] Latin has "Ptolemy."

[2] Possibly because the malefic planets rule the last bound in all 12 signs.

[3] Meaning: Directing in zodiac degrees (1˚ in the zodiac = 1 year in life) rather than in right ascension or oblique ascension of the zodiac, as Ptolemy advocates. According to Ptolemy, direction is done in equatorial degrees with one

succeeded. [21]

Know that when two aspects of malefics join together in one degree, they will not cut off life, for the nature of one is the opposite of the nature of the other,[1] so they will only produce illness, and according to the influence of the [stronger] one so will be the nature of the illness.

THE SECOND HOUSE

Ptolemy said that we should always look to the rulers of the triplicity of the sign where the Sun is if the nativity is by day, and if by night, we should look to the triplicity rulers of the sign where the Moon is, and according to the influence of each one of them so will be the period allotted to the ruler of the triplicity.[2] And this is true, since the place of the Sun by day [is where] we can take the measure of life from, and so you should do [with the Moon] by night.

[Sources and Timing of Material Benefit and Wealth]

Doroneus said that we should always look to the superior planets in the nativity, and if we find one of them oriental of the Sun [and] in its greatest strength,[3] we shall observe over which one of the houses in the wheel it has dominion, and from that we shall know in which way benefit will come to the native. We shall always take the house it aspects, and leave

---

equatorial degree equals one year. When the prorogator is closer to the M.C., it should be directed by right ascension, and when closer to the Asc. or Desc., it should be directed by oblique ascension. In either case one degree of the zodiac may equal less or more than one year of life depending on the prorogator's sign and the geographical latitude of the nativity. See *Tetrabiblos* Book III, chapters XI – XV (Ashmand, 88-100).

[1] A cancellation effect, possibly because Saturn is cold and somewhat moist and Mars is hot and dry. Not certain whether the statement is true for a bodily conjunction only.

[2] Not found in Ptolemy, but mentioned by Dorotheus, book I, chapter 24, 184ff. A method of evaluating the general well-being and overall quality of life, by dividing it into three major periods, each described by the condition of the current triplicity ruler of the prevailing luminary – the Sun by day and the Moon by night.

[3] That is when the separating angle from the Sun is increasing before the superior planet turns retrograde.

the other house. If it aspects both [places, then] benefit will come from both of them, and if one of the houses is of the nature of the planet, then much benefit will come by way of that house.[1] If the superior planet is a benefic, then the benefit will come with no fear and with no trouble. But if the planet is a malefic, the goodness will come with worry and fear.

Likewise we shall observe the inferior planets, whether one of them is occidental of the Sun and in its greatest strength. If so, it will indicate benefit that comes from its houses and it will [also] come from the house that it aspects.

If Jupiter is in one of the pivots or in the eleventh house, not under the light of the Sun, and not retrograde, then it also indicates much benefit and wealth and money. If it is in the first house or in the tenth house, this will come about before the middle of life, and if it is found in the remaining pivots, it will come about after the middle of life. If Jupiter is oriental of the Sun before its first station or opposite the Sun [moving] towards [22] its second station, the person will have honor and wealth before the middle of life; if [found] in the remaining two quadrants, it will come about after the middle of life. According to its strength such will be the person's wealth.

All this is [so] if Jupiter is the ruler of the nativity, the ruler of the hour of the nativity, the ruler of the house of the Sun by day, or of the Moon by night. If it does not have dominion over the places I have mentioned, it will do little good. You should also observe that [even] if it is in its greatest strength vis-à-vis the Sun, or in the ascendant, or in one of the other pivots, and [at the same time] it is in its house[2] of detriment

---

[1] The translation of the previous phrase is uncertain as it is not clear exactly which houses are discussed here. It is possibly a reference to the circumstance when two signs/houses that are ruled by one planet. [Additional by RH] The Latin here is so different that it cannot serve as a guide. Here is the whole thing from "benefit will come to the native." ... *et ab eo sciemus unde nato bonum continget. Et semper domus est accipienda* [text has *accidenda* which is an obvious typo] *secunda: et quod eam aspiciat: et dimittere domum aliam.* "and from it we will know whence prosperity will happen for the native. Always one must take the second house and what aspects it, and disregard any other house."

[2] The word 'house' is used in this instance in the sense of a sign that is ruled by a planet according to a mode of rulership, i.e., domicile, exaltation, or triplicity. It does not mean 'house' in the conventional sense of a division of the chart into first house, second house, third house etc. These latter were each originally called a 'place', in Greek *topos* (τόπος), Latin *locus*. The Greek word for 'house' was *oikos* (οἶκος). This word was used exclusively for signs of the

or fall, it will decrease the benefit that the triplicity indicates, for these three things are principal.

If a malefic [planet] is in one of the pivots, it indicates bad [things], and if it is oriental of the Sun, the affliction and adversity will come before the middle of his life, and if occidental, [it will come] after the middle of his life. Also, observe which pivot it is in, as you did for the benefic planet.

Doroneus said that a planet above the earth indicates the first half of a person's life, and the one under the earth will indicate the second half. Abu Mashar said that the Lot of Fortune indicates the first half and the ruler of the house of the Lot of Fortune indicates the second half. Abu Ali[1] said that the Moon indicates the first half and the ruler of the house of the Moon [indicates] the second half. Al Andruzagar said that we should always observe the planets that aspect the Moon and divide life according to them. This is a proven thing, for when the native completes the number of years that is equal to the ascension of the sign where the malefic is [found], at the number of the[se] years the harm and affliction will come to him according to the nature of the planet, the sign it is in, and its relation with the Sun. The reason for this will become clear in the example that I will give. Saturn's nature indicates all illnesses. [23] One time it will indicate constipation and another time it will indicate diarrhea for when

---

zodiac as signs in which planets had rulership, that is, the same way that 'house' is used here. An ambiguity seems to have arisen when these words were translated into Arabic which used two different words for our 'house' in astrology, *bayt* which means 'house' as sign, more or less as used here, and *qisma* which means 'house' as 'place', or 'house' as used in astrology from the later middle ages forward. In Hebrew and Latin both of these words were translated with a single word for house in Hebrew בַּיִת *Ba'it*, and in Latin *domus*). See Jennifer Ann Seymore, *The Life of Ibn Ridwan and His Commentary on Ptolemy's Tetrabiblos*, Doctoral Dissertation, (Columbia, 2001), 264-5. Also see Abu Ma'shar, *The Abbreviation of the Introduction to Astrology*, ed. and trans. Charles Burnett , K. Yamamoto & M. Yano (Leiden; New York; Koln: E. J. Brill, 1994), 155 where the Arabic *bayt* is defined as equivalent to the Latin *signum*, meaning 'sign'. From here on in this text when the word 'house' is followed by word patterns such as "of exaltation," "of detriment," or "of fall," it is a sign that is referred to, not a house or place as in first house, second house, etc. When otherwise unqualified, 'house' will continue to refer to one the places. This terminological ambiguity has caused much difficulty for both historians and astrologers. [RH]

[1] The Latin says 'Welius' here rather than Abu Ali.

it is ascending in its greater wheel,[1] it will indicate constipation, and when it is descending, it will indicate diarrhea. When it is in the first quadrant vis-à-vis the Sun, which is from the time of its rising [before the Sun] until its first station, it is warm and moist; [from] its first station to the opposition of the Sun, it is warm and dry; if it is from the opposition of the Sun to its second station, it is cold and dry; from its second station until it becomes hidden under the light of the Sun, it is cold and moist. (Similarly,) if it is between the line of the mid-heaven and the rising degree, it is warm and moist; from the line of the mid-heaven to the setting degree, it is warm and dry; if it is between the setting degree and the lower pivot, it is cold and dry; if between the lower pivot and the rising degree, it is cold and moist.

Sahel the Israelite said that if it is between the beginning of its elevation in its greater wheel[2] whose solid [wheel] is far from the solid [wheel] of the earth, it is cold and dry until ninety degrees [in the wheel]; from ninety degrees to the place of descent, it is cold and moist; from the place of descent to ninety degrees, it is warm and moist; from there to the [place of] elevation it is warm and dry.

You should always observe the sign where Saturn is, for if the nature of the sign is warm, it will decrease [Saturn's] coldness, and if it is cold, it will increase hurt upon hurt. And what I said for Saturn, such is the way of Jupiter and Mars.

Only the inferior planets – from the time they become visible above the earth and are occidental, their nature is warm and moist. It is so for the Moon until her [first] quartile aspect to the Sun, and for the inferior planets until their first station. For the rest of the quadrants, do as I have shown you. In the same way that you observe Jupiter, you should [also] observe Venus; for if it is in one of the pivots, or in the fifth house which is its house of Joy, it indicates [24] the good [things] with no trouble nor fear but with joy and contentment. The benefit will be according to its strength and according to the influence of whatever rulership it has.

As a rule when the Sun is by day in its house of exaltation and it is in one of the pivots, in the eleventh house, or in the ninth house, which is its house of joy, it will also indicate benefit, honor, and eminence.

Likewise, if the nativity is by night and the Moon is in her house of exaltation, in one of the pivots, in the eleventh house, or the third house

---

[1] Probably the Deferent. [RH]
[2] According to the Latin, this is the eccentric. [RH]

which is her house of joy, she will indicate benefit, honor and wealth.

Similarly, any planet that is in its house of exaltation, the good that it indicates will be according to its nature, such as Jupiter which indicates [high] office and trust, and Saturn [which indicates] buildings, and Mercury [which indicates benefit] from sciences and skill, and Venus from women, and Mars from wars, and the Sun from kings.

[Ptolemy's Ages of Life]

Ptolemy said that[1] the Moon will serve the native [for the first] four years, and according to the influence of the Moon at the moment of birth and in the annual revolution so will be the health of his body. Mercury will serve ten years after the Moon, and according to its influence at the moment of birth and in the annual revolution so will be the matters of his studies and skills. Then Venus will serve for eight years, and according to its influence at the moment of birth and in the annual revolutions so will be his lust in the matters of women. Then the Sun will serve for nineteen years, and according to its influence at the moment of birth and in the annual revolutions so will be his authority and rank. Then Mars will serve for seven years,[2] and according to its influence at the moment of birth and in the annual revolutions so will be his effort and work to gain wealth that will last for the end of his life. Then Jupiter will serve for twelve years, and according to its influence at the moment of birth and in the annual revolutions so will be his worship of God. Then Saturn will serve until his death, and according to its strength at the moment of birth and in the annual revolutions so will be his movements and his heaviness (of movements) and the health of his body in old age. This Ptolemy said, but did not give a reason for this division. So here is the reason for the [period

---

[1] This next paragraph is based on Ptolemy's division of time as applied to the ages of life, (Book IV, chapter X, Ashmand, 138-139). First he states the need to "... pre-determine the appropriate fitness of every age to such events as may be expected....", then says "The mode of consideration applicable to human nature is universally one and the same; and it is analogous to the arrangement of the seven planetary orbs. It therefore duly commences with the first age of human life, and the first sphere next above the earth, that of the Moon; and it terminates with the final age of man, and the last of the planetary spheres, which is that of Saturn. ..."

[2] Possible mix-up: 'seven' is the Mars number in the Firdaria system. [Additional by RH] This should be 15 both according to Ptolemy and the Latin.

of the] Moon; [it is the time] until the child is weaned and four years have passed, as each year it is under the influence of one sign until the completion of four signs that represent the four elements.[1]

We shall give [both] Mercury [25] and Mars half of their minor years,[2] and to the Sun, the Moon, and Jupiter we shall give each one according to its minor years.

The Persian and Hindu astrologers rely on the division called al-Firdar, as I shall explain in [the chapter on] the revolutions at the end of this book with the help of God.

[Additional Considerations for Wealth]

Masha'Allah said that if the ruler of the second house is in the rising sign, one will gain profit and wealth without effort, but if the ruler of the rising sign is in the second house, one will work hard to pursue money; therefore look to see if that planet is one of the benefics [for] then the person will not lack for anything, only it will come with an effort. If it is one of the malefics and it is in its house of rulership, [the native] will squander his money on his own accord, but if the malefic planet is not in its house of rulership, the money will be taken from him against his will, secretly such as in stealing, or in the open such as by robbers that attack him. If the ruler of the second house is under the light of the Sun and Jupiter is in a bad place, [the native] will always be poor.

You should also look at the Lot of Fortune, for its influence is the same as that of the second house; every planet that aspects it will indicate money according to its nature.

If the ruler of the second house gives its power to the ruler of the rising sign, even from youth the native will have money without effort. If the ruler of the rising sign gives its power to the ruler of the second house, his livelihood will come with effort, and if the ruler of the second house is in one of the pivots, he will find money; if in a falling house, [he] will not be able to make a living except meagerly.

Al Andruzagar said that the first ruler of the triplicity of the second

---

[1] Ptolemy says: ". . . Hence, the first age of infancy, which endures for four years, agreeing in number with the quadrennial period of the Moon, is consequently adapted to her; being in its nature moist and incompact, presenting rapidity of growth, being nourished by moist things, . . ." (Ashmand, ibid.)

[2] The Latin only refers to Mercury in this respect. Mars gets 15 years. [RH]

house will indicate the first one third of the native's life, the second ruler [of the triplicity] will indicate the middle [one third], and the last one will indicate the last [one third of life].[1]

THE THIRD HOUSE

[Siblings]

Doroneus said that if the rising sign is Capricorn or Cancer, then the native will have quarrels with siblings. The reason for this is known since [26] the ruler of the third house is [also] the ruler of the twelfth house which indicates quarrels.[2] In the same way you will figure all the signs, for if the rising sign is Aries or Libra, the native will cause his own death[3] and will have money from women, and he will have a chronic illness in one of his limbs, and he will rejoice with his father for the nature of the Moon and the Sun is the same,[4] and he will have arguments in a foreign country

---

[1] Presumably these refer to the state of one's substance in each of these periods, but neither the Hebrew nor the Latin make this explicit. [RH]

[2] Capricorn on the ascendant puts the domiciles of Jupiter (Sagittarius and Pisces which are in a square to each other) on the cusps of the 12th and the 3rd houses. When Cancer is rising, the domiciles of Mercury (Gemini and Virgo) create the same condition. Here, and in the text that follows, Ibn Ezra draws attention to an interpretation principle derived from the fact that each planet rules two signs. Such pairs are known as Same Engirdling signs.

[3] With Aries rising Mars also rules Scorpio on the 8th house cusp, and with Libra rising Venus also rules Taurus on the 8th house cusp. This creates what can be called a union between these houses. Only Mars and Venus can do that because they rule quincunx (150° apart) signs. This also creates a connection between the ascendant and the 6th house when Taurus or Scorpio are rising. Note that both Jupiter and Mercury rule square signs, and can thus create a union between angles, which a very desirable condition.

[4] This may be derived from the fact that elsewhere Ibn Ezra says that the Sun and the Moon always receive each other, which means that they have power in each other's domicile. Reception also creates a union. A possible interpretation is: With Aries rising the Moon rules cancer in the 4th house of fathers and the Sun, which has dignity of exaltation in the ascendant, also rules Leo in the 5th house – the house of pleasure and enjoyment, which trines the ascendant. With Libra rising we have Saturn ruling Capricorn on the 4th cusp and Aquarius on the 5th trine the Libra ascendant where Saturn is dignified by exaltation.

or with inn keepers[1] [variant text: "or with learned people"]. If the rising sign is Taurus or Scorpio, the native will bring illnesses on himself; he will have quarrels with women, and money from land, and most of his friends will die. If the rising sign is Gemini or Sagittarius, his siblings will destroy his money, and [he] will make money from things that are laid away as treasures; most of his children will become his enemies. These things do not require explanations for they are taken from the relationship between the houses that belong to a single planet. In the same way [you should] derive the rest of the rules [for the signs] that I did not mention.

If you find the ruler of the third house in a trine or sextile aspect with the rising degree or with the ruler of the rising sign, there will be complete harmony between the native and his siblings, and if it is an opposition or quartile aspect, there will be enmity and competition between them. You also ought to look at Mars, for it rules siblings in every nativity,[2] and if it is in an opposition or square aspect with the rising sign or its ruler, the native will fight with his siblings. You can know which one of them will win according to the strength [of the planets] as I shall explain in the chapter on the seventh house when I mention matters of adversaries. If Mars beholds the Lot of Fortune in a harmonious aspect, [the native] will have benefit from his siblings, and if it is a bad aspect, loss of money will come through them.

Ptolemy said that Saturn and the Sun indicate brothers that are older than the native, Jupiter and Mars indicate the middle ones, and Mercury [27] indicates the young ones. The Moon indicates the older sister and Venus indicated the younger one, and according to their influence and their relation to the rising sign and its ruler so will you judge for each one of them.

Doroneus said that you should always look to Mars, and according to its influence so are the affairs of the brothers. And look to see if it is oriental of the Sun; [then] it will always indicate the older ones; if occidental, it will indicate the younger ones. If Mars, the ruler of the third

---

[1] With Aries rising Jupiter rules the 9th house of travel and the 12th house, and with Libra rising Mercury does the same thing.

[2] In *The Book of Reasons* Ibn Ezra has the scheme by which Mars signifies siblings because it is in the third sphere of the heavens counting from Saturn down. Apparently the number 3 is the connection to the 3rd house. [Additional by RH] This scheme is found in many other works as well. See Johannes Schoener, *Three Books on the Judgment of Nativities,* Book I, translated by Robert Hand (Reston, VA: ARHAT Publications, 2001), passim.

house, and the ruler of the Lot of Brothers[1] are in one of the Water element signs,[2] judge that the native will have many siblings;[3] if the three of them are in barren signs, the native will not have siblings; and if some are in the Water element signs and some in the barren signs, this will indicate an average number. According to the majority so you will judge. If Mars is under the light of the Sun, and so is the ruler of the third house and the ruler of the Lot [of Brothers], all the native's siblings will die in his lifetime, and if not all three [indicators] are like that, some will live and some will die.

If the Lot [of Brothers] is in a male sign, and the ruler of the lot is oriental of the Sun or in one of the quadrants of the wheel which are male and in a male sign, and the third house is in a male sign and the ruler [of the third house] and Mars are in male places, [then] the native will not have sisters but brothers [only]. If it is the reverse, [meaning] that they are all [in] female [places], [then] it will be the opposite; and if some are [in] male [places] and some are [in] female [places], they will be [some of] this and [some of] that. If these three that indicate siblings are all in double-bodied signs, the native will have siblings from another father or another mother.

[Faith]

Astrologers [also] look to this house as an indicator of religions;[4] thus, if Jupiter is in this house and the nativity is by day, the native will be insincere for he will appear to people as righteous but he is not so. If the Sun is there and it rules the nativity, it will indicate that [the native] has no faith at all. [28]

If the Moon is there and the nativity is by day, the person will be a true believer;[5] if by night, the person will also be righteous, except that he

---

[1] The lot of Brothers is taken by day and by night from Saturn to Jupiter and cast from the Ascendant.

[2] The Hebrew here actually says 'houses' but this is another instance of the sign-house ambiguity referred to earlier.

[3] Water signs are fruitful.

[4] The 3rd house is called 'Goddess' and the 9th house is called 'God'.

[5] The 3rd house is the Joy of the Moon.

will show more than what is in his heart,[1] and if Jupiter is there by night, he is also a righteous person.[2] All this is [so] if Jupiter is not combust or retrograde.

If you find one of the malefics in the third house, they will indicate a liar. If Mercury is there and it is configured with one of the malefics, it will indicate one who falsifies records and is a perjurer.

You should look, [both] by day or by night, to the Lot of the Sun,[3] for if the lot, or the ruler of its house if aspecting (the lot), is in the sign of the Great Conjunction [and this sign is also] in the share of the nation the native belongs to, and the ruler of the house of the lot is retrograde, or in the sixth house, or in the twelfth, the native will abandon the religion of his forefathers and will turn to another religion.[4]

Venus in this house indicates upright faith if not combust by the light of the Sun or retrograde.

It is the same (positive indication) when the ruler of the third house in one of the pivots, in its power, and in harmonious aspect with the ruler of the rising sign.

If the ruler of the rising sign is there, in its power and not aspected by one of the malefics, then the native will worship God and his dreams are true and do not require interpretation.[5]

---

[1] The preceding phrase is not clear: רק יותר יראה מה שיש בלבו. It may also be understood as "he will show more of what is in his heart." Either way, this seems to come from the fact that the Moon, which rules by night, indicates things that are hidden, not visible.

[2] That will place Jupiter in the right sect.

[3] Also known as the Lot of Spirit, or Divinity, and is associated with the 9th house. The diurnal formula is from the Moon to the Sun, added to the Ascendant, and reversing the Sun and the Moon by night.

[4] This is an interesting connection between the chart of the individual and the Great Conjunction which is usually observed for mundane historic events and the destiny of nations and the collective.

[5] These attributes actually belong in the 9th house. It could be either due to text corruption or intentional, since the 3rd house is called "goddess" and also has "divine" attributes, as the opposite and the complementary of the 9th house which is called "god'.

THE FOURTH HOUSE

[The Father and His Measure of Life]

Ptolemy said that we should always look to the place of the Sun in the nativity, whether by day or by night, and from it we could know the number of days [of life] of the [native's] father remaining from the day of birth [of the native].[1] He said that if the Sun is in conjunction with Saturn, or in opposition or quartile aspect with Mars, it indicates longevity for the father. If the Sun is in conjunction with Mars, or in opposition or [29] quartile aspect with Saturn, it indicates his (the father's) short life.[2]

This notion is not true, for the malefics will always indicate evil, whether by conjunction, by opposition, or quartile aspects, and only the benefic planets will indicate good. A quartile aspect is better than a conjunction, for [in a conjunction] their power weakens under the light of the Sun.

For the one born by day direct the place of the Sun to an abscission place according to the rules for directions that I have shown you. We will also direct Saturn to an abscission place, and we will also direct the cusp

---

[1] The native's father is one of the significations of the 4th house. Ptolemy, who typically does not use the signification of houses in the traditional way, uses the Sun by day, and Saturn by night, as the significators of the father in the chart.

[2] Ibn Ezra's source may have been corrupted. Here is the quote from the *Tetrabiblos*, Book III, chapter V (Ashmand, 78-79) with regards to the effect of the malefics on the life of the father:

"The probable duration of the lives of the parents . . . in the case of the father, a long life is presaged, if Jupiter . . . or also, if Saturn himself makes a harmonious configuration with the Sun; (that is to say, either by conjunction, the sextile, or the trine;) provided that such configuration be fully and strongly established and confirmed:- and, when not so established and confirmed, although it does not actually denote a short life, yet it will not then equally presage a long life. . . . If however the planets be not posited in the manner just described; . . . And if Mars be elevated above, or ascend in succession to the Sun, or to Saturn; or, even, should Saturn himself not be in consonance with the Sun, but configured with it by the quartile or opposition, . . ." [Depending on the house placements, the father will suffer injuries, disease, infirmities and a short life.] The quote continues: "And, if Mars be aspected to the Sun in the way before-mentioned, the father will die suddenly, or receive injury in his face or eyes; but, should Mars be so aspected to Saturn, he will be afflicted with . . . or even death may be the consequence. And even Saturn himself, if badly configured with the Sun, will also inflict disease and death on the father . . . incidental from watery humour."

39

of the fourth house in the steps[1] of the right wheel,[2] as well as the place of the Lot of the Father,[3] wherever it is, to the abscission [place] that is before it.[4] At the time when two testimonies join together, then the father will die.[5]

The opinion of the astrologers is that we should look, by day, to the place of the Sun, and if it is in one of the places of life that are mentioned in [the chapter on] the First House, and it is aspected by one of the rulers of its place[6] while the ruler is in its great[est] power vis-a-vis the Sun[7] and the rising sign, [then] the father will live according to the mean number of years of the aspecting [planet]. If [that planet] is not in its greatest power, he will live according to the minor years of the aspecting [planet]. If the Sun is not in a proper place, or it is in a proper place but no ruler is aspecting, then take Saturn instead of the Sun and do accordingly. If the measure of life cannot be taken from Saturn, [then] take it from the Lot of the Father, and if you cannot take it from there, take it from the [cusp of the] fourth house.

If the nativity is by night, you shall begin from Saturn, then the Sun, then the fourth house and lastly the Lot of the Father, and do accordingly. And the verity of the directions is a tried (tested, proven) thing.

If one of the malefics is in the domicile of the Sun, [whether] by day

---

[1] See page 72, note 1 for a discussion of 'steps' versus 'degrees'. [RH]

[2] The term is *'galgal ha'yosher'* (גלגל הישר), which can be read as 'the straight wheel', and is probably the equator, and therefore, the reference is to direction in right ascension.

[3] From *The Beginning of Wisdom* chapter 9: ". . . the Lot of the Father taken by day from the Sun to Saturn and the reverse by night, and cast from the rising [degree]. If Saturn is under the light of the Sun, then it is taken by day from the Sun to Jupiter, and the reverse by night, and cast from the rising [degree]." (*The Beginning of Wisdom*, 143).

[4] 'Before' can be understood as 'ahead or behind it in the order of the signs'. I tend to think it's 'ahead', so the direction is done forward. [Additional by RH] The Latin has the same thing, *Et iterum ducas locum partis patris in queM.C.unque sit locum ad abscissionem que est ante ipsum.* "And again you direct the place of the Part of the Father, in whatever place it may be, to an abscission which is before it.

[5] As more than one astrological indication is needed in order to bring about such a severe event.

[6] The condition called "reception."

[7] This would be in an opening arc phase with the Sun – dexter aspect for Mars, Jupiter and Saturn, or sinister aspect for Venus and Mercury.

or night, at the moment of birth, it will harm the father in his eyes, or his measure of life; if one of the benefics is there, his life will be long. [30]

As a rule when the Sun alone, or Saturn alone, or the Lot of the Father alone, or the [cusp of] the fourth house reaches an abscission place, it indicates sickness and harm that will come to the father according to the nature of the abscissor planet.

Know that there is a controversy between Ptolemy and [other] astrologers, for he says that the tenth house signifies the father and the fourth house signifies the mother,[1] and the [other] astrologers say the opposite. Al Nirid[2] said that if the nativity is by day, we should assign the fourth house to the mother and the tenth to the father, and if by night, we should reverse it. Sabanu[3] said that if the fourth house is in a male sign, it indicates the father, and if female, it indicates the mother.

The truth is [in] the words of the [other] astrologers, and here is the principal [reason for] this controversy; for when we direct the fourth house to an abscission place, at the same time the tenth house will [also] reach an abscission place.[4] So if we cannot know the measure of the father's life from the Sun, nor from Saturn, nor from the Lot of the Father, but [only] from the fourth house, [and] [if] also we cannot know the measure of the mother's life from Venus, nor from the Moon, nor from the Lot of the Mother, but only from the tenth house, then the father and the mother should die at the same time. And this is the reason for the controversy.[5]

Similarly, if we take the measure of the native's life from the Sun as well as the father's life, it is possible for the Sun to come to an abscission place and at the same time one of the [other] four places of life of the native [comes] to an abscission place, and so does the degree of the fourth house or the Lot of the Father or the place of Saturn; then the father and the son (the native) will die on the same day. Likewise, if two of the places of life of the native reach an abscission place, and at the same time

---

[1] This is another instance where Ibn Ezra refers to something from Ptolemy that Ptolemy did not in fact say. [RH]

[2] Latin has "Al-Kindi" here. [RH]

[3] Latin has Sabach. We have no idea who this is. [RH]

[4] If one forms a conjunction, the other forms an opposition, and a square to one forms a square to the other.

[5] In other words, according the rules laid out, both parents would die at the same time when the 4th house or the 10th house are afflicted by directions. Without further qualifications from the other indicators of the parents we are still unable to distinguish between these two angles as to which parent they signify.

the place of the Moon by night and also by day if she qualifies [as an indicator] to know the measure of life from), and at the same time if Venus, or the degree of the tenth house, or the Lot of the Mother reaches an abscission place, [then] the native and his mother will die in one day.[1]

---

[1] This whole passage is organized rather differently in the Latin but seems to amount to the same thing. Here is the Latin and a translation:

Et radix huius discordie est. Quoniam cum ducimus domum quartam ad locum conscissionis una est per copulam coniunctam et alia per aspectum attinget. Et tunc si non poterimus scire locum quantitatis vite patris a sole: neque a Saturno neque a parte patris: sed totum a domo quarta.

Itidem si non possimus scire quantitatem vite matris a Venere neque a luna a parte matris: sed totum a domo decima: tunc morietur pater et mater in uno tempore.

Et ideo occurrit discordia inter sapientes signorum.

Et similiter si accipimus quantitatem vite a sole: et vitam patris ab eo. Poterit namque contingere quod attingit locus solis ad locum conscissionis. Et sic uno tempore morietur pater et filius: et eodem modo cum acceperimus quantitatem vite nati et matris a luna morietur simul natus et mater. Et similiter in aliis: et attiget isto tempore locus lune in nocte.

Et iterum in die: si hoc scitur quanta est quantitas vite nati: illa hora attinget Venus aut gradus decime: aut pars matris [Latin edition has *pars martis* which is clearly an error.] *ad locum conscissionis: morietur* [Latin text has *movetur* which is also clearly an error] *natus materque eius die una.*

And the root of the disagreement is this. Because when we direct the fourth house [cusp] to the place of abscission, in the one case it is by means of a conjunctional linkage and in the other case [the opposite house cusp] arrives by an aspect. And this, then, is if we are not able to know the place of the quantity of the life of the father from the Sun, nor from Saturn, nor from the Part of the Father, but rather completely from the fourth house [cusp].

In the same manner, if we cannot know the quantity of the life of the mother from Venus, nor from the Moon, nor from the Part of the Mother, but completely from the tenth house [cusp], then the mother and the father will die at the same time.

And on this account, the discord has occurred among the sages of the signs.

Also, likewise if we take the quantity of life of the native from the Sun and the life of the father as well, it can indeed happen that the place of the Sun will reach the place of abscission and in this manner the father and son will die at the same time. Also, in the same manner, when we take the quantity of the life of the native and the mother from the Moon, the native and mother will die at the same time. Also likewise in other instances a place

Yaacov Al Kindi said that we should always look, by day and by night, to the place of the Sun, Saturn, the fourth house and the Lot of the Father, and we shall seek the ruler[s] of these four places, and according to the influence of the ruler so will be the matter of the father.

If the ruler is in its greatest strength in the nativity but weak in one of the annual revolutions, it will indicate harm that comes to the father according to the division[1] of the houses where it is [found].

The important thing is that you should assign the fourth house as if it is the rising sign of the father, and from there take the portion of the houses as they are divided in the nativity according to the latitude of the location. I shall give you an example. Consider the rising sign at the moment of birth as three degrees of Cancer in the beginning of the fifth region;[2] then the fourth house will be eight degrees of Virgo and the fifth house will begin at twelve degrees of Libra. Then you will assign the rising sign of the father [from] eight degrees of Virgo, and not from three [degrees of] Libra which is the beginning of the fourth house in the number of degrees [counted] in the signs, since the steps of the right wheel (the equator) are the principal ones.[3]

In this way you should direct every year sign [after] sign, beginning from eight [degrees] of Virgo, and you could know the death of the father from the nature of the abscissor of life of the father according to its place and the planets aspecting it.

As a rule if you find in the fourth house any of the planets, whichever it may be, make it co-participant to know the matter of the father. It is so

---

will reach [the place of abscission] in this time in the night.

And in turn in the daytime, if it is to be known how great the quantity of the native's life is [from Venus, the tenth house cusp, or the Part of the Mother], in that time that Venus, or the tenth house cusp, or the Part of the Mother reaches the place of abscission, the native and the mother will die on the same day.

I think this organization is a bit clearer than what seems to have come from the Hebrew. [RH]

[1] Latin has *participationem,* 'sharing' or 'participation' [RH]

[2] Also known as 'clima' plural 'climata'

[3] This is a clear statement in favor of unequal houses, at least in terms of the chart angles. This particular example fits a chart run with Placidus houses for 43 north latitude.

in the nativity and in every annual revolution.[1]

[Land and Property]

This house indicates land in the nativity of every person, and only in the nativity of kings will it indicate the countries the king rules over. If the ruler of the fourth house is in one of the pivots, not burnt by the Sun and not retrograde, the native will buy land; and [32] if the ruler of the fourth house beholds the ruler of the nativity [by] a friendship (harmonious) aspect, [the native] will find profit and all benefits from land; if it beholds [the nativity ruler] in a hostile aspect, there will be quarrels because of land; if he (the native) is a king, the people of country will conspire against him. You will be able to know who will win according to the strength of the ruler of the nativity, especially if it is a superior planet, as I shall explain in the chapter on wars in *The Book of Elections*.[2]

Also look to the Lot of Land[3] and the planets that aspect it, and according to what you see judge for good or bad. Always observe Saturn [to see] if it is strong vis-a-vis the Sun and the pivots and [whether] it has dominion in its place and [whether] it rules the nativity; then he will like buildings and start new plantings. It is the same when the ruler (of the nativity), whichever it is, is in the fourth house and in its power, and also if it is in one of the Earth signs.

[The End of the Matter]

This house indicates the end of every matter; so, therefore, if a benefic planet is there, not retrograde, not combust and not in its house of fall or detriment, then the native will have a good end [of life].

Abu Mashar said that the ruler of the house of the Moon will indicate

---

[1] The Latin seems to have run this section together with the next section omitting the reference in the next section to the fourth house indicating land. This looks like an omission in the Latin. This could be a clue to which manuscript the Latin was based on, or it could be a simple error by the translator. Omissions are a common type of transcription error. [RH]

[2] The section "and if the native is a king . . . ruler of the nativity . . ." is omitted in the Latin. The following section is also garbled in the Latin. [RH]

[3] From *The Beginning of Wisdom* chapter 9, 143: "The fifth is the Lot of Property (land) taken by day and by night from Saturn to the Moon, and cast from the rising [degree]."

the end of [life of] the native.

Al Andruzagar said that the first ruler of the triplicity of the fourth house, as calculated according to the latitude of the location and not according to the number of degrees in the signs, signifies the father and the second ruler of triplicity signifies the land, and the last ruler of the triplicity indicates the end of the native.[1]

The ancients said that if Mars or Saturn are in the fourth house and it is not one of the domiciles of the benefic planets, and no benefic planet is aspecting, it indicates that after the native is buried they will disinter him from his grave.

Enoch said that if there is a benefic planet in the fourth house, [33] or the ruler of the fourth house is in a good place and it gives its power to the ruler of the second house and it is in a good place, not combust and not retrograde, it indicates that the native will become rich from a treasure he will find. You could know when this would come about in the native's life by observing the ruler of the second house, whether it is oriental of the Sun or occidental, and in which quadrant of the pivots, and if it is above the earth or below it, as explained in the book *The Beginning of Wisdom*.

THE FIFTH HOUSE

[Children]

Enoch said that we shall always look to the ruler of the fifth hour from

---

[1] It seems that a scribal error led to the following manuscript text: "the ruler of the first triplicity of the fourth house, ... signifies the father and the ruler of the second triplicity signifies the land and the ruler of the last triplicity indicates the end of the native". This does not make astrological sense, as a house has one sign i.e. belongs in one triplicity. The triplicity has three rulers, which in this scheme govern the different functions of the house. This error is repeated for the rest of the houses and seems consistent across the manuscripts. The translation here was modified to correct this. Most likely, the "original" scribe erroneously attributed the number 'first' *rishona* (ראשונה) the word for 'triplicity' *shalishut* (שלישות) (feminine) rather than to the word for 'ruler' *ba'al* (בעל) (masculine) which should have been '*rishon*' (ראשון) so it became השלישות הראשונה בעל rather than בעל השלישות הראשון.

45

birth,[1] and from it we could know the matter of children. And in the same way he said that the ruler of the first hour from the birth signifies the native; the ruler of the second hour signifies the money; the ruler of the third hour signifies the siblings; and the ruler of the fourth hour signifies the father. According to the strength of each one so will be the matter it indicates.[2]

All the ancients agreed, and Ptolemy among them, that Jupiter indicates children, and according to its strength in the nativity so will be the children.[3] You have to observe its place, for if it is in a barren sign, he will have few children, and the opposite if it is in one of the water signs. If it is oriental of the Sun in the first or tenth pivot, he will have children before the middle of his life, and the opposite if it is occidental of the Sun and in the other pivots. If it is in a male quadrant,[4] oriental of the Sun, and [in] a male sign, most of his children will be male, and the opposite if [Jupiter is] in opposite [conditions]. If Mars conjoins it, or is in bad aspect to it, most of his children will die.

Al Kindi said that you should always observe the place of Jupiter, [34] the fifth house and its ruler, the ruler of the fifth hour, the ruler of the Lot of Children, and observe who is the ruler of these places (having the most dominion), and observe if it is in a conjunction or aspect with the ruler of the nativity; [then] he will have children, and if not, there will not be [any].

Enoch said that before you look into the matter of children you should observe whether he is ready (able) to have children. He said that it is a tried (proven) thing that if Venus is in Leo,[5] burnt by the Sun, and it is the ruler of the nativity, he will never have children because of a defect in his

---

[1] This most likely refers to the ruler of the 5th temporal hour after birth. The word is 'nolad' (נולד), meaning 'born' or 'newborn', and can also be taken as 'the native' or 'the nativity', but if read as 'molad' (מולד) – it would mean birth.

[2] The Latin says exactly the same thing as the Hebrew. This is a most peculiar and interesting doctrine. [RH]

[3] While this makes sense, the Latin has "tenth house" not Jupiter. While Ptolemy does look at the tenth for children, Jupiter is usually considered to be the planet that signifies children the most of all planets. *The Beginning of Wisdom*, 95. [RH]

[4] The quadrant from the Asc. to the M.C. and the one opposite it.

[5] Leo is one of the barren signs.

46

member, and likewise if it is in Scorpio.[1] The rule is that Venus indicates the dripping[2] and according to its strength and weakness you will judge.

[The Number of Children]

Ptolemy said in the *Book of Four Chapters* that we should always look for the matters of the child from the tenth house and from the eleventh house,[3] and all those that came after him, and Masha'Allah among them, ridicule him and they are right. I have mentioned this to you so that you don't rely on all the things in that book, for there is no validity in it. For [example] he mentioned in his book that if the Sun and the Moon are in a double-bodied sign, or if the Moon, or the Sun, or the rising sign are in double-bodied signs, the native will not be alone in the belly for there will be twins. And this is a great error, for the Sun stays for one third of the year in double-bodied signs and the Moon is in double-bodied signs one third of the month,[4] so all the time that the Sun is in those signs one third of the newborn should be twins. We have also seen many nativities where the luminaries are in double-bodied signs and all the five planets and the rising sign as well, and the native did not have a twin with him. And he [also] said that it is possible to know whether the native is firstborn to his father or not; for if Saturn is found in one of the pivots of the nativity, it is a reliable testimony that the native is the firstborn.

Likewise, if the ruler of the rising sign [35] is in the third sign (house)[5] and it is of the superior planets, and likewise if the ruler of the third house is in the rising sign and it is of the inferior planets, and likewise if the first ruler of the triplicity [of the third house] is in the rising sign, [then] the native will be the firstborn. Yet, we have seen more then ten children that have all these [indications] come together in their nativity and none of them was the firstborn. And another thing [he said] that it is possible to know the number of children; for when Jupiter or Venus aspect the tenth or eleventh house and they are in a double-bodied sign, it will

---

[1] Scorpio rules the reproductive organs and is the place of detriment for Venus.

[2] Semen.

[3] The Latin has *a domo septima et .5.* "from the seventh and the fifth house . . ." This is clearly wrong, but that is what is written. [RH]

[4] The Latin omits "and the Moon . . . one third of the month, . . . " It looks as though it should be there [RH]

[5] Latin here has *signum* "sign" throughout. [RH]

indicate two [children], if in a fixed sign, one [child] and if in [a] changeable, [sign] three. Similarly, he said that he could know the number of the native's wives[1] from the place of Venus and the Moon.

The truth is what Enoch said, that it is not possible to know the [exact] number of children or wives, but only whether they are many or few. Therefore, if you found the book of Sahel the Jew on nativities, do not rely on it for it has many such [sayings] that have no principle (foundation) and examination will refute them.

Al Andruzagar said that the first ruler of the triplicity of the fifth house indicates the first children, the second ruler of the triplicity indicates the middle ones and the third ruler of the triplicity indicates the young ones, and you should always assign Mercury[2] as a co-ruler together with it.

[Pleasure]

We have already mentioned that Venus rejoices in the fifth house, so every nativity that has Venus there, and it is not combust and not retrograde, and has no bad aspect from a malefic planet, then he will have children as he wishes, and he will delight in them.

Venus [in this house] also indicates that all his life he will enjoy food and drink, and many gifts that are brought to him, especially if Venus rules the nativity.

THE SIXTH HOUSE

[Health]

Observe if the native was born by day and [whether] the Sun is in one of the pivots with a malefic planet or its aspect; [if so] it indicates harm in the right eye. If the malefic is in a sign of human form, the cause of the harm is from a blow of a person, and if in the maimed signs, which are Aries, [36] Taurus, Cancer, and Scorpio, as well as Capricorn and Pisces, the harm will be from an illness according to the nature of the malefic [planet]

---

[1] 'Wives' is not present in the Latin, but the Latin does not make sense here. [RH]

[2] Mercury signifies children and young people in general.

and the place it is in. In a diurnal nativity, if the Moon is in the seventh house, or tenth, and in a bad aspect with one of the malefics, there will be a defect in his left eye. If both luminaries are this way, the defect will be in both his eyes.

If the Moon in a diurnal nativity is in the other houses and aspected by one of the malefics, or the Sun is like that, it will not indicate complete damage in the eye; if the Moon in under the earth in a diurnal or nocturnal nativity, it will indicate illness in the lung or in the upper organ (stomach), and not in the eye at all. It is a proven thing that if the Moon is under the earth in a diurnal or nocturnal nativity, the native will have a coughing disease; and if the Moon is in a nocturnal nativity in bad configuration with the malefics and she is above the earth, it will indicate harm and defect in the right eye.

Know that the Sun indicates half of the person's body, and that is all of the right side, and the Moon [indicates] the left side; if both luminaries are strong, no illness will befall him in either side. If one of them is in bad aspect with Saturn, he will be afflicted by tremor and plague in the side that it indicates. If the malefic is Mars, and it is in a human sign, know that the harm will come from a person by means of a blow or a sword.

Know that Saturn indicates the right ear, [both] by day and by night; so if it is above the earth, it indicates disease in the ear if it is burnt by the Sun or in bad aspect with Mars or Mercury; and if it is so under the earth, he will have the disease of the spleen.

Jupiter indicates the left ear; so if it is burnt by the Sun or it is in bad aspect with Saturn or Mars or Mercury, especially if it is in the sixth house, it will indicate pain in the left ear, [both] by day and by night.
And Enoch said that it is not so, only if it is above [37] the earth in a diurnal or nocturnal nativity; if it is under the earth in this configuration, he will have a disease in the liver.

Mars indicates the right nostril if it is above the earth [both] in a diurnal or nocturnal nativity, and [when] Mars is combust or in a bad aspect with Saturn and Mercury, [it indicates disease in the nose],[1] and if [found] under the earth in the same configuration, it indicates [disease] in

---

[1] The rule here seems to be that when the planet is above the earth and afflicted, then the ailment will be in the upper organs ruled by the planet, and if below the earth, in the organs of the lower part. Based on this understanding, the phrase in parentheses was supplemented. [Additional by RH] The same omission occurs in the Latin text.

the gallbladder.[1]

Venus indicates the left nostril, so, in a diurnal or nocturnal nativity, if it is above the earth and in a bad aspect with the malefics, or combust, it indicates disease in the left nostril; and if below the earth, it will indicate disease in the [sex] organ or the dripping.

All this that I have mentioned is true, and the ailment indicated by the planet or the luminary will become obvious if it is the ruler of the nativity.

Know that Mercury indicates the tongue by day and by night, whether it is above the earth or below the earth. So if it is in a conjunction with Saturn and there is no latitude between them, or in a bad aspect with it, and Mars is not aspecting it,[2] especially if the ruler of the nativity is Saturn or Mercury, there is no doubt that the native will be a stutterer. [Also] if Mercury is in this configuration and in one of Saturn's domiciles, and even more severe if it is in the sign of Pisces, [for then] it indicates that the native is mute.[3]

[For] all these ailments that I have mentioned, do not judge them to be so [only] because of the malefics that aspect; for if the benefic planets aspect, and they are stronger than the malefics, they will remove the ailment until it is not seen at all (anymore), or cover it so it is not visible.

Masha'Allah said: Observe whether the rising degree is the place of the Pleiades, or the Moon is there in a bad aspect with one of the malefics; this indicates eye disease.

In general, if the ruler of the sixth house is one of the malefics and it aspects the rising degree, the ruler of the rising sign, or the ruler (of the chart), it indicates illness and pain. You could [also] know which ailments are indicated by [the placements of] the planets in the signs, [38] as I have mentioned in the book *The Beginning of Wisdom*.

If the malefic is oriental of the Sun, the deformity will be permanent, and if occidental, it will not last.[4] You ought to observe if the malefic is in a fixed sign, [for then] it indicates a long illness, and if in a changeable [sign], it indicates that it will go away quickly, and if a double-bodied

---

[1] The word is '*mrira*' (מרירה) which seems to mean 'bitterness'. In *The Beginning of Wisdom*, chapter four, 98, he says that Mars rules the gallbladder, which in Hebrew is '*marah*' (מרה), also meaning 'bitterness'.

[2] 'Not' is present in the Latin. This reading from the Hebrew appears to be correct. [RH]

[3] Water signs have no voice.

[4] Mars and Saturn are superior planets which are considered strong when oriental of the Sun before their first station.

sign, it indicates that he goes from one illness to another.

Ptolemy said that if the ruler of the sixth house is with one of the malefics, or in a bad aspect with it in the sixth house, it indicates chronic illness, and if in the seventh house, it indicates bleeding from the rear.[1]

Abu Ali[2] gave a rule [that] if the ruler of the sixth house is in the sign of Aries, it indicates illness in the head, if in Taurus, in the neck, [and so on], the way it is written in the book *The Beginning of Wisdom.*

Masha'Allah says that the rising sign indicates the head and all the [other] houses [follow] by way of the division from Aries.[3]

Ptolemy says that the rising sign indicates the heart, the tenth house the head, the seventh the feet and the fourth the bottom of the person, and this is a proven thing. Whatever Abu Ali said, as mentioned above, is also true.[4]

Enoch said that if the distance between the Sun and Saturn, or Mars, whether oriental or occidental of it, is 82 degrees,[5] it indicates harm in the eye.

You should always observe the Moon since she indicates the body, for if she is with Saturn and her light is decreasing, it will indicate an illness that comes from cold; if her light is increasing, it indicates little illness; if she is with Mars and her light is increasing, it will indicate serious illness because of the added heat, and if her light is decreasing, the illness will be light. Know that the nature of Mercury is to increase,[6] so

---

[1] It looks like another attribution falsely attributed to Ptolemy. Also, it is possible that he is referring not to Ptolemy directly but to Haly Rodan's Commentary or something of the sort. [RH]

[2] The Latin refers to "Welius." [RH]

[3] The Latin for this and the next section is also a mess. Here is what it says, *Messahac quoque dicit signum ascendens significare: caput septimam: pedes quartam inferius hominis: et hoc est expertum. Et itidem idem quod welius asserit est expertum.* "Messahalla also says that the rising sign signifies the head, the seventh the feet, the fourth the lowest part of a human. And this has been found [to be true.] And likewise, that same thing which Welius asserts has been found [to be true.]" The reader is advised that in the punctuation system used in the Latin text the colon ':' does not mean what it means in modern punctuation. It is also possible that the Latin represents a confusion between this and the next passage in the Hebrew. [RH]

[4] See the end of the previous note. [RH]

[5] Within the orb of a square aspect.

[6] This is an unknown Mercury attribute. Possibly used here because Mercury takes on the nature of the planet it is configured with.

51

you should observe its aspect to the Moon. Know that the aspect of the Moon to the Sun, whether a trine or a quartile or a sextile, is better than [39] the aspect of Jupiter or Venus;[1] for if the two malefics are with the Moon, the influence of the Sun's aspect will remove their power.

[Slaves]

Know that this house signifies slaves; so if the ruler of the sixth house is in a conjunction or aspect with the ruler of the nativity, he will have slaves, and according to the aspect of the ruler [of the house] to the rising [degree] so you will judge whether they (the slaves) will be useful or cause damage.

If the ruler of the sixth house is in the tenth house, it indicates that the native will [be] control[led by] his slave in his mind and in his money;[2] if the ruler of the sixth house is in one of the signs of human form, his slaves will be obedient; if the sign is male, it indicates that the male [slaves] are better for him than the female ones, and the opposite if it is in a female sign.

Al Kindi said: Always observe the sixth house and the place of its ruler and the place of Mercury, which signifies slaves, and the Lot of the Slaves,[3] and see which is the [strongest] ruler of these places, and according to its strength you will judge.

Al Andruzagar said: The first ruler of the triplicity of the sixth house indicates the deformities, the second ruler of the triplicity [indicates] the ailments, and the third ruler of the triplicity [indicates] the slaves.

THE SEVENTH HOUSE

[Marriage of Men]

Ptolemy said that if the Moon is under the light of the Sun and Venus is

---

[1] A very intriguing statement. [Yes! The Latin agrees. RH]

[2] A slightly different and intriguing variations from PAR1056: "If the ruler of the sixth house is in the tenth house he (the native) will put his slave in charge of his mind and his money."

[3] The *Lot of Slaves* is taken by day and by night from Mercury to the Moon, and cast from the Asc..

in a bad place such as the sixth house or the twelfth, or is retrograde, or Saturn is beholding it in a bad aspect, it indicates that the native will not have a wife all of his life.

Enoch said: Always observe Venus, the Moon, the Lot of Wives,[1] and the seventh house and its ruler; see which is the [strongest] ruler of these places, and if it conjoins, or is in any aspect whatever with the ruler [of the nativity, then] he will have wives, and according to the strength of the ruler so will they be.

It is known that every [40] nativity that has Venus or Mars as its ruler while they are conjoined, or one beholds the other in any aspect whatever, and Jupiter does not aspect them, this indicates an adulterer.

If Venus is the ruler and it is burnt by the Sun, or in a bad aspect with Saturn, especially if it is in one of its (Saturn's) domiciles, or in the sign of Virgo, which is Venus' sign of fall, it indicates illicit intercourse practices that are improper.

Observe if Venus is in the twelfth house or in the seventh house;[2] he will always have quarrels with women or because of them. It is the same if the ruler of the seventh house is in a bad aspect with the rising sign or its ruler, or with the ruler of the nativity.

If Venus and the Moon and the ruler of the seventh house are in signs of beauty, his wives will be beautiful, and the domiciles of Saturn indicate the opposite.

If Venus and the Moon are occidental of the Sun, especially if one of them is in one of the domiciles of Mercury, it indicates young [wives]. The domiciles of the superior [planets] indicate older [wives].[3]

A bad aspect to Venus from Saturn indicates widows; a bad aspect

---

[1] From *The Beginning of Wisdom*, 144: "The Lot of Marriage for men and women is taken by day and by night from Venus to the setting degree, and cast from the Ascendant.

"The *Lot of Marriage in the Nativity of Men* according to Enoch taken by day and by night from Saturn to Venus, and cast from the Ascendant, and according to Valens taken by day and by night from the Sun to Venus, and cast from the Ascendant."

[2] Typically, when bad things are indicated, the 12th house goes together with the 6th house, so the 7th house here looks like an anomaly, or a scribal error. However, no variant has been noticed. [The Latin also has *in domo duodecima aut .7...* "in the twelfth house or the 7th". RH]

[3] The Latin has *parvitatem* "smallness" and *granditatem* "largeness" instead of "young" and "older." However, the Hebrew makes more sense, and even the Latin could be interpreted this way metaphorically. [RH]

from Mars indicates divorcees or raped ones, and Jupiter indicates virgins. Know that if Venus confers its power to Jupiter, it indicates that [the native] will be righteous in the ways of intercourse and will not commit a transgression.

If Venus, the Moon, and the Lot of Wives, taken according to Enoch, are in moveable signs,[1] they indicate many wives, and the opposite if in fixed signs.

The [general] rule is: Look to Venus, for according to its influence and its aspect to the rising [degree] or its ruler, so will be the benefit that comes from the wives, or the damage. And always include with it the ruler of the seventh house; for if this ruler, or Venus are in the second house, it indicates that he will inherit from his wives.[2]

Ptolemy said: If you find Venus, or the ruler of the seventh house in one of the pivots, it indicates that he will take a wife [41] from his [own] family. And if the ruler of the seventh house, as I have mentioned, is in the third house or the ninth, it indicates that he will take a wife in a foreign land, or a foreign wife in his [own] country.

[Marriage of Women]

Masha'Allah said: In a woman's nativity observe the place of the Sun for it indicates her husband as the Moon indicates wives in the nativity of males, and according to the influence of the Sun so will be her husband. So if the Sun is in conjunction with Saturn, or in bad aspect with it, and Venus is combust or retrograde, especially if it is in the sixth house or the twelfth, she will not have a husband.

Al Kindi said: In the nativity of a woman observe the place of the Sun, Mars, the seventh house and its lord, and the Lot of Males,[3] and know which is the [strongest] ruler of these places, and according to its

---

[1] The manuscript text says "in signs of the water element." The Water signs in general indicate fruitfulness and multiplicity. The change is suggested by Robert Hand: This could be textual corruption here. [Additional by RH] The Latin has . . . *in signis mobilibus: significat uxores multas. Et econtrario si fuerint in signis fixis.* " . . . in moveable signs, it signifies many wives, and the contrary if they are in fixed signs." This makes more sense.

[2] The Latin has here . . . *ipsum habiturum hereditatem propter eius uxorem.* " . . . he will have an inheritance because of his wife." [RH]

[3] *The Beginning of Wisdom*, 145: "The thirteenth is the *Lot of Bridegrooms* taken by day and by night from Saturn to Venus, and cast from the Ascendant."

influence so will be the husband. If the ruler is oriental [of the Sun], he will be young in years, and if occidental, the opposite, and according to the nature of the ruler so will be the nature of the husband.[1] If the Sun is in its domicile or its exaltation, she will have a husband from a great family and he will have a high rank, and the opposite if the Sun is [in] the opposite [condition].

In this way you will judge the nativity of the males. If you see Venus in its house of fall and likewise the Moon, it indicates that he will take a wife from a family inferior to his own, and if the opposite, he will take a wife from a family more noble than his family.

Always observe in the nativities of [both] males and females, if Mars is in the seventh house, there will be divorce between them, especially if it is the ruler of the nativity or the seventh house.[2]

Al Andruzagar said that if Venus is in the ninth house, it indicates that he will leave his wife, and this is true if Venus is the ruler of the nativity.

[Quarrels]

This house signifies wars; so if the ruler of the seventh house is in a bad aspect with the ruler of the rising sign or its ruler, it indicates that he will have many quarrels with people according to the nature of the ruler of the seventh house. If it is Saturn, [42] it indicates quarrels with old people and with inferior people and slaves; if Jupiter, it indicates quarrels with judges and the people of faith; if Mars, it indicates quarrels with thieves and robbers; if the Sun, his wars will be with kings and ministers; if Venus, it indicates the women and the eunuchs; if Mercury, it indicates the learned and the scribes; and if the Moon, it indicates all [common] people.

If the ruler of the nativity and the ruler of the seventh house are conjoined and you wish to know who will win, look to see which of the planets is closer to its elevated position vis-a-vis the solid wheel;[3] it will overcome the one that is distant from its elevated position. Likewise, also observe [which] one of them is closer to its elevated position in the small

---

[1] This sentence is missing in the Latin but it certainly is in accord with the tradition. [RH]

[2] The Latin has *nona* "ninth". This does not make sense. It may also be a copyist error because of what follows. [RH]

[3] Basically 'the solid wheel' is right except that the Latin refers to the *augis respectu circuli ecentrici* "eccentric circle" rather than the "solid wheel" and the stronger planet is the one closer to its apogee, i.e., elevated position. [RH]

wheel (the epicycle) for it will overcome the lower one.

Observe if one is in the ecliptic and the other is northern; know that the northern one will win, especially if one is northern and the other is southern [of the ecliptic].

If both are northern, observe the one that has more latitude, [for] it will overcome that one whose latitude is smaller.

If both are southern, the one whose latitude is less than the other's will always win.[1]

The planet that is direct in motion will overcome the one that is retrograde.

The planet that is aspected by the Sun will overcome the one that is combust or under the light of the Sun.

The planet that is in its place of dominion will overcome the one that is in a place where it has no dominion.

If the two planets are not conjoined but have an aspect between them, observe the one in the tenth house [for] it will overcome the one in the other three pivots, and the one in the first house will overcome the one in the two [remaining] pivots, and the one in the seventh house will overcome the one in the fourth house.

If one of the planets is a superior and the other is an inferior, the superior one will always overcome the inferior one. There is no need to mention whether they are both superior or both inferior, for this is not possible because of the division of the domiciles since the domiciles of Saturn are opposite the domiciles of the Luminaries, the domiciles of Jupiter are opposite the domiciles [43] of Mercury, and the domiciles of Mars are opposite the domiciles of Venus.[2]

You should calculate the numbers of all the [types of] victories that I have mentioned, and the one whose number is the highest will triumph over the other, and I shall explain this in *The Book of Questions*.

[Partnership]

This house also indicates partners, so if Mars is there, it indicates that the

---

[1] The general rule is that the planet that is relatively more northern – measured in ecliptical latitude – overcomes the one below it.

[2] All pairs of opposite signs are ruled by a superior planet and an inferior plane, so when the ruler of the 1st and the 7th form a conjunction, by definition one will be a superior and the other an inferior.

partners will deceive him and steal his money; (but) if the ruler of the second house is in a good aspect with the ruler of the seventh house, it indicates that he will profit by the partners.[1]

Al Andruzagar said: The first ruler of the triplicity of the seventh house indicates the wives, the second ruler of the triplicity indicates the quarrels, and the third ruler of the triplicity indicates the partners; according to the strength of each one so you will judge.

THE EIGHTH HOUSE

[Death]

As a rule if the ruler of the nativity confers its power to the ruler of the eighth house, all his life the native will be in worry, desolation, and fear of death. Likewise, if the ruler of the eighth house is in a bad aspect with the malefics, it indicates many troubles and great dangers that will befall that native.

If you find the Moon in the eighth house with a malefic planet or in aspect with it, it indicates unnatural death according to the nature of the malefic and the place it is in. Mars indicates getting killed or being devoured by animals. Saturn indicates drowning if it is in a sign of the water element or in the sign of Aquarius,[2] and if in a sign of the earth element, it indicates a wall that will fall on him. If the ruler of the seventh house[3] is in the ninth place, it indicates that he will fall from a high place

---

[1] The Latin has the following: *Quod si fuerit in domo secunda in bono aspectu: aut sit dominus* [reading *dominus* for *domus*] *septime: hic denotat ipsum habiturum lucrum participationum.* "But if he [Mars] is in the second house in good aspect, or he is the ruler of the seventh, this denotes that the native will have profit from his partners." The Hebrew makes better sense. [RH]

[2] In the tropical zodiac Aquarius is classified as an Air sign. Yet, Saturn, its ruler, traditionally signifies sailors and sea captains, and sidereal Aquarius has water in it as it is associated with the constellation of the Water Bearer which is connected with the river where the Piscean Fishes swim.

[3] The text has 7th house, but it seems to me it should be 8th. This connection between the 7th house and the 9th house in the context of death does not make astrological sense: It comes under the heading of the 8th house, not the 7th. The 9th traditionally had no 'death' indications, except in the context of travel. The "high place" is not a 9th house signification either. However, no variant text has been noticed as yet.

and die.

It is the same rule for the Moon if it is with one of the malefics in any place whatever, but you will not accept her testimony alone until you seek the testimony of the ruler of the 7th house.[1]

Ptolemy said that if the luminaries are in Gemini or Pisces, and one of the malefics is with them or in bad aspect to them, especially if the rising sign is one of those signs, it indicates that the hands and the feet of the native will be cut off[2] and he will be hanged on a tree. And if the ruler of the places of death is in the sign of [44] Gemini [joined] with Mercury, he will fall from a high place and will die.[3]

These are the places of death: The eighth house and the place of its ruler, the Lot of Death,[4] and the place of the Moon, and from the ruler of these you will know the nature of death.[5]

If Mars is the ruler of death and it is burnt by the Sun, kings will kill him; if it is in one of the water signs, he will die because of scalding water; and if in signs of human form, he will die by the hand of robbers. If the Sun rules death and it is in the seventh[6] or sixth house, he will die an unnatural death together with many other people. If Venus is the ruler of death and it is in a bad aspect with one of the malefics and Venus is in one of the water signs, he will die because of poisoning. If Saturn is the ruler [of death] and it is in its inferior place[7] and retrograde, he will die of diarrhea and if in [its] elevated place he will die of constipation. If Jupiter

---

[1] Here too, the text has 7th house, which is probably a scribal error. [Additional by RH] The Latin also refers to *domo septima* the "seventh house".

[2] Gemini rules the hands and Pisces the feet. [Additional by RH] It's the Ptolemy problem again!

[3] Possibly because the Air element signifies higher elevation in the sequence of Earth, Water, Air and Fire.

[4] *The Beginning of Wisdom*, 145-6: ". . . the *Lot of Death* is taken by day and by night from the degree of the Moon to the beginning of the eighth house, . . . and cast from the place of Saturn."

[5] The Latin is slightly different: . . . *domus octava locus eius domini: pars mortis locus lune: et principans super ista: ab his quidem scire poteris mortis maneriem.* ". . . the eighth house, the place of its lord, the Part of Death, the place of the Moon, and the ruler of the Moon; from these you can know the manner of death." [RH]

[6] Latin has *in domo octava* . . . "in the eighth house . . ." [RH]. A possible explanation for the 7th house: It is the place of connection with other people. [MBE]

[7] The Latin makes it clear that "perigee" is referred to. [RH]

is the ruler [of death] and it is in a bad aspect with the malefics, he will die from excess of blood.

Enoch said that if the ruler of death is Venus or Mercury and they are in their first station, the native will die an unnatural death; if they are in the maimed signs,[1] he will die from unusual diseases; and if the ruler of the eighth house is in a good place and not aspected by a malefic, he will die in his bed from an illness that will come according to the division of the signs, where Aries signifies the head[, etc.]

Do not judge from its testimony alone, and always look at the place of the Moon, and whether there is a malefic in the eighth house.

If the ruler of the eighth house is aspecting its house, the native will die in his [own] country except when it is in the twelfth house, or in a place that does not aspect its [own] house; [then] he will die in a foreign land.

If the ruler of the eighth house is in the sign of Scorpio and is aspected by one of the malefics, a dog will bite him and he will die; if it is in the sign of Leo, he will be devoured [by an animal]; and if there is a benefic planet [45] in the eighth house, he will be saved from any unnatural death.

Ptolemy said: He whose [rising] sign is Aries or Libra will cause his own death or kill himself, and the reason for this is that the rising [sign] and the eighth house are [ruled by] one planet.

Sahel the Jew said that he had seen in the *Book of Secrets* by Enoch that the one born at the end of Pisces will die in fire,[2] and if Saturn is in the eighth house and [the sign is] of the water element, he will die in water, and if in an earth element, he will die in a landfall (landslide or building collapse).

Al Kindi said: Look at the eighth house and the nature of the sign and which planet is with it or aspecting it, the place of the ruler of the house, the place of the Moon, and the place of the Lot of Death, and know which is the ruler of these places; according to the place of the ruler you will judge. If the ruler is in its house of dignity and no malefic planet is aspecting except that it is under the light of the Sun, he will die suddenly

---

[1] Al-Biruni (Ramsay trans., 212): "Aries, Taurus, Leo and Pisces are described as maimed, the first three because their feet are cut off at the hoofs and claws , and Taurus in addition because it is only half an ox, cut in two at the navel, while Pisces is included on account of the absence of limbs."

[2] Possibly due to the presence of a fixed star.

but will not feel [it coming] until he dies.

[Inheritance]

Ptolemy said that if the ruler of the eighth house is of the benefic planets and it is in the second house, not combust and not retrograde, he will inherit money from ones who bequeath it to him. It is the same judgment if the ruler of the second house confers its power onto the ruler of the eighth house that receives it and[1] if it (the ruler of the eighth) is in one of the good houses.[2] It is the same judgment if the Lot of Fortune is in the eighth house and joined with a benefic planet.

Al Andruzagar said that the first ruler of the triplicity of the eighth house indicates death, the second ruler of the triplicity indicates inheritance and the third ruler of the triplicity indicates worries (and fears), and according to the strength of each one of them so you will judge.

THE NINTH HOUSE

[Faith]

If Jupiter is in this house and it is not burnt by the Sun, not retrograde and there is no malefic planet beholding it in a bad aspect, and the nativity is by day, the native will be God fearing and his faith will be complete, especially if it is in a fixed sign, and more so if oriental of the Sun.

If Jupiter is [46] the ruler of the nativity, he will leave all [worldly] affairs and will seclude (dedicate) himself to worship God. If it is so in a nocturnal nativity, he will show himself humble but will be a hypocrite.

If Saturn or Mars are in the ninth house, it indicates one who is deceitful in his faith and lies under oath, except when the native is Jewish [for then] Saturn will harm less, but Mars will harm so that [the native] will [eventually] excommunicate himself.[3]

---

[1] The phrase here is not 'and', but 'so that', which does not clearly connect to the preceding part of the sentence.

[2] Latin has *in domo fortune* " in the house of a fortune." [RH]

[3] In Al-Biruni's *The Book of Instruction In The Elements of The Art of Astrology* (Ramsey trans., 253), under the section "Indications as to Religions, Pictures of Planets," we find planetary association with religions: "Saturn: Jews and those who dress in black. . . . Jupiter: Christians and those who dress in white,

Always look at the Lot of the Sun, which is the Lot of Mystery,[1] [and] if you find it in a Jewish nativity in the sign of Aquarius, and in a Christian nativity in the sign of Leo, and [in the nativity] of a Moslem in the sign of Scorpio, and the ruler of the Lot is retrograde, [the person] will leave his religion, and this is a proven thing.

Venus in the ninth house indicates faith mixed with love and desire. The Sun in this house indicates good faith for it is in its house of Joy,[2] and it indicates that he will rise to a high rank because of his faith and righteousness.

The opposite of this is the Moon, for it indicates harm that will come to him from lack of faith.[3]

Enoch said: Observe the place of the ruler of the ninth house and according to its influence so will be the faith of the native, and if Mercury is there, it indicates that his learning is greater than his faith. If the Moon is in the third house,[4] whether by day or night, it indicates a person fond of religions (or studies) and laws.

[Dreams – Prophetic]

Saturn in the ninth house indicates the verity of one's dreams, and the opposite of this is [when] Mars [is there]. The Sun also indicates true dreams,[5] and according to the nature of the planet that you find in the ninth

---

... Mars: Idolaters, ... Sun: Wearing a crown, Magians, Mithraists. ...Venus: Islam. ... Mercury: Disputants in all sects. ... Moon: Adherents of the prevailing religion. ..."

Therefore, according to this scheme, for a Jewish person Saturn is proper in the 9th house will not cause loss of faith. Mars will cause excommunication because if idolatry and heresy.

[1] Also known as the Lot of Spirit, Lot of Hidden Things, Lot of Prophecy, Divinity. It is taken from the Moon to the Sun by day, and the reverse by night, and added to Ascendant. It is one of the lots of the ninth house, even though not listed under that heading in *The Beginning of Wisdom*.

[2] In this case "house of" refers to a house, not a sign. [RH]

[3] Possibly because the 9th house is the opposite of the 3rd house which is the Joy of the Moon.

[4] OX707 has: 'the ninth house'.

[5] The text appears to be '*mehuvanim*' (מכוונים), which would mean 'intended' or 'purposeful', but, assuming a scribal error, it makes more sense to read it as '*nehonim*' (נכונים), which means 'true', as in 'true prophecy'. Prophetic dreams are one of the attributes of the ninth house. [Additional by RH] This

61

house such is most of the matters of the dreams of the native.

[Travel]

Enoch said: If you find Saturn in the ninth house, it indicates trouble that will come to him at sea or in the rivers, especially if it is in a water sign. If Mars [is there] instead of Saturn, it indicates great trouble that will come to him on land from robbers. And according to the strength of the ruler of the ninth house so will be the outcome whether at sea or on land.

If a retrograde planet is in the ninth house, it indicates a person inconstant in his faith, especially if it is in a changeable sign. [47]

[Science and Learning]

This house indicates the sciences. The science of Saturn is measurements (geometry); the science of Jupiter is religions (philosophy); the science of Mars is medicine;[1] the science of the Sun is the law;[2] the science of Venus is music; the sciences of Mercury are the grammar of language, logic, philosophy, and mathematics, and it partakes in all [the other] kinds of sciences; the Moon indicates knowledge of stories and tales.[3] And I have already discussed in the [chapter on the] First House how you can tell whether the native will be learned or not as compared to his parents.

---

statement about the Sun is omitted in the Latin.

[1] The connection of Mars (and Venus) with medicine is mentioned by Ibn Ezra in the context of the 6th house in *The Book of Reasons*.

[2] Oddly enough the Latin has for the Sun, *solis scientia sunt iudicia astrorum.* ". . . the science of the Sun is the judgment of the stars. [RH]. That fits with the prophecy and prophetic dreams, mentioned above. [MBE]

[3] Latin has: *verba inana et reprehensionem.* ". . . empty words and censure." [RH]

THE TENTH HOUSE

[The Mother]

If the nativity is by day and Venus is in one of the pivots or in the eleventh house, and is not combust, and one of the rulers of its place is aspecting it, you can know the life of the mother from the moment of birth (of the native). Look at the ruler of the place of Venus [and] if it is in one of the pivots and not combust and not retrograde, it indicates that the mother will live the mean [number of] years of the planet, and if it is not in one of the pivots, she will live according to the number of its minor years, and this is the theory.

The main thing is that you should direct the place of Venus to an abscission place as I taught you in the directions of the places of life.

If Venus is not [in] a proper place take the Moon instead, and observe if one of the rulers of her place is aspecting her, and do according to the [above] judgment.

If [you can]not [take] the Moon in this way, seek the Lot of the Mother[1] and do according to the [above] judgment.

If that is not proper, direct the beginning of the tenth house to the place of abscission.

If the nativity is by night, begin from the Moon, then Venus, then the tenth house, then the Lot of the Mother.

Al Kindi said that we should always look to the ruler of the [afore]mentioned places, and according to its strength so will the mother live.

Masha'Allah said: In every nativity for the father look to the Sun and Saturn, and for the mother to the Moon and Venus, and whichever is closer to an abscission place, [that parent] will die first.

[Rank and Honor]

This house indicates kingdom, dominion and honor. If you find the Sun in this house, especially if it is in its domicile or house of exaltation, it is an indication of [48] the height of the native's rank. Similarly, if the Sun confers its power onto the ruler of the nativity and it is in one of the good

---

[1] The *Lot of the Mother* is taken by day from Venus to the Moon and the reverse by night, and cast from the Ascendant.

houses,[1] then he will serve kings and they will love him. If the ruler is under the light of the Sun and is not in the sign of Leo, nor in Aries, he will serve kings but they will eventually harm him and torture his feet in chains; if one of the malefics is aspecting [these two], the kings will kill him.

If Saturn is in the tenth house in a diurnal nativity, especially if it has dominion over the nativity, or it is in one of the pivots, it indicates the high rank to which the native will come after 30 years have passed. If the nativity is by night he will always have fear and harm because of kings.[2]

If Mars is in the tenth house by day, great fear and terror will befall him from military commanders, and if by night, he will have rank with the military commanders; he will get into dangers,[3] and will escape.[4]

If Mercury is in the tenth house, he will have honor because of his knowledge, and if Venus [is there], because of a high ranking women, and the same is for the Moon, and if Jupiter [is there], because of the law and learning and faith.

And here is a rule I shall give you. Always observe [that] if you find in the nativity one of the planets that is in its house of exaltation, not retrograde, not in conjunction with one of the malefics, nor in bad aspect with them, [then] observe which house it has rulership over and from that place honor will come to the native.

If [this planet] is the ruler of the nativity [and also] the ruler of the first house, the person will be respected by all people and will be proud of himself and of his beauty (looks).

If it is the ruler of the second house, the person will earn money through kings.

If is the ruler of the third house, the person will have honor because of one's brothers or relatives.

If it is the ruler of the fourth house, the honor will be from the status of one's family and from hidden things.

If [it is] the ruler of the fifth house, one will have honor because of one's children.

---

[1] Latin has *domorum fortunarum* "houses of fortunes" [RH]

[2] By day Saturn, a diurnal planet, in this position would be in the right sect, and by night would be out of sect.

[3] Latin has *carcerem* "prison." [RH]

[4] Mars, being a nocturnal planet, is harmful if it is in the same hemisphere with the Sun by day, and the angular position only amplifies that. In the 10th house by night, it is in the right sect relation.

If [it is] the ruler of the sixth house, for one's slaves.

If [it is] the ruler of the seventh house, for one's wives.

If [it is] the ruler of the eighth house, the person will have honor at the time of death.[1]

If [it is] the ruler of the ninth house, [the honor will be] for one's faith and learning.

If [it is] the ruler of the tenth house, [the honor will be] for one's trade. [49]

If [it is] the ruler of the eleventh house, [the honor will be] because of one's success and one's friends.

[The Hebrew text is missing for the twelfth house. The Latin adds, "and if it is in the twelfth house, he will be honored by his enemies and because of the riding of animals."][2]

[Profession and Skills]

Astrologers have composed many books to know the trade of the native, and I shall give you a general rule for them. Always look to Mars and Venus and Mercury and observe their places, and whether they aspect one another, and in what sign they are. For if they are in water signs, one's trade will be in ships and anything that is goes in water,[3] and if in the fire signs, one's trade will be silversmith or blacksmith, and if in the air signs, one's trade will be in people's needs,[4] and if in the earth signs, one will be a builder or a digger.

The main thing they said is that Mars indicates swiftness and endurance of the toil and [hard] work, and Mercury indicates all the crafts and Venus indicates the perfection[5] of the craft, and according to the influence of each one of them such will be his strength in his trade.

If Mars alone [indicates] the trade, and it is in its house of exaltation,

---

[1] Latin has *propter mortuorum hereditates*. "because of inheritances from the dead." [RH]

[2] *Et si dominus .12. honorabitur ab inimicis suis et propter equitationem animalium.* [RH]

[3] Latin has: *in omnibus rebus viventibus in aqua.* "all things living in/on the water." [RH]

[4] Latin has: *eius artificium instruere homines.* "his skill is to instruct people." [RH]

[5] The aesthetic aspect of work, or completion.

it indicates a warrior and a robber, and if in its house of fall, he will be a blood letter (or: blood spiller).[1]

If the ruler of the nativity is Mercury, it indicates that one's trade is by science if Mercury is not retrograde, for if it is retrograde, it indicates a tailor or a one who sews.

And they also said that Saturn does not indicate a skill because of the sluggishness of the native except when it aspects the ruler of the trade.

And this is how you know the place of the ruler [of the trade]. Look to the place of Mars, Venus, and Mercury, and see which is the ruler of those places, and that one will be called the ruler of the trade. If it co-mixes with Saturn, it indicates a dirty occupation, such as a tanner or parchment maker. If both of them are in earth signs, he will be a grave digger.

Jupiter does not indicate a trade, for it seeks other worldly pursuits, except when it aspects the ruler of trade, [then] it indicates great profit and wealth that he will receive for his trade, and all his dealings are in matters of religion and law.

The Sun does not indicate trade either because of its haughtiness, except when it beholds the ruler of trade in a good aspect [then] most of his trade will be in the house of kings. [50]

The Moon does not indicate trade because of its stupidity.[2]

Enoch said: If you find the ruler of trade combust, or retrograde, or in the sixth house, or in the twelfth[3] house, and no planet is aspecting the Moon, the native will be a beggar.

Ptolemy said: Always observe the planet that is oriental of the Sun, and according to its nature and the nature of the sign it is in, and the nature of the [planets] aspecting it, such will be the trade of the native; and he spoke correctly.

---

[1] Latin has *falsificator* "liar." [RH]

[2] No offense to anyone, but the rationale is that the Moon has nothing of its own, since it reflects the light of the Sun, which makes it an imitator. Previously he says that the talent of the Moon is in repeating, or telling stories of what it has heard.

[3] Some of the texts say 11th (י"א) house, and some say 12th (י"ב). 12th makes sense since all the preceding attributes are negative, and so are the indications of the 12th house, whereas the 11th is a fortunate house.

If you find in this house one of the superior planets, especially Jupiter, and it is not retrograde, nor combust, it indicates a person successful in all his undertakings. And if the ruler of the second house confers its power to a planet in this house, [the native] will profit in trade and in any occupation that he does.[1]

If Venus is in this house, he will profit but little, and worries will follow every gain.

If the Moon is in this house, the native will be loved by all people. It is so [too], if the ruler of this house is in its greatest power and is beholding the rising sign or its ruler in a harmonious aspect; if it is a hostile aspect, it will be the opposite.

If Saturn is in this house, and it is in a sign where it has dominion, it indicates that most of his friends will be old people and lowly and dejected people, unless it is in its house of exaltation, or oriental of the Sun.

If Jupiter is in this house, most of his friends will be judges,[2] philosophers, and be trustees of treasures.

If Mars [is in this house] and it is in its house of exaltation, his friends will be ministers and mighty warriors, and if in its house of fall, his friends will be robbers and thieves.

Enoch said: Observe in every nativity whether Mars is beholding the ruler of the nativity in a bad aspect, or the ruler [51] of the nativity is in the sign of Scorpio; [then] it indicates that the native is a thief.

If the Moon is opposite Mercury and they are aspected by Mars in any aspect whatever, and they are in one of the pivots, there will be no occupation for the native but thievery.

If the Sun is in the eleventh house, most of one's friends will be kings and famous people; if Venus, they will be women and eunuchs; if Mercury, most of one's friends will be the learned and the writers; and if the ruler of this house is in the eighth house, it indicates that most of one's friends will die in his lifetime.

---

[1] The eleventh house is the Joy of Jupiter. It is also called 'Acquisition', and has financial and material indication as second from the tenth house.

[2] Latin has "*iudei*" which means "Jews" but this is obviously a typo for "*iudices*,"judges. [RH]

[Imprisonment and Captivity]

Observe whether the rising sign, or a planet in the rising sign, confers its power to Saturn in the fourth house, [for then it] indicates that the native will be in jail or in captivity for many years.[1]

Likewise, if the ruler of the ninth house is burnt by the Sun in one of the pivots, it indicates that [the native] will be kidnaped on the road and go into captivity.[2]

Also, if the ruler of the nativity is in the sixth house or the twelfth, it indicates that his enemies will capture him.

And now I will reveal a secret to you, mentioned by Ptolemy, [who] said that if a benefic planet rules an evil house, it will not indicate good; such as Jupiter; if ruling the house of enemies, it indicates that the judges will sentence him to whipping in justice, for he has transgressed; and if the ruler is a malefic planet, he will be wronged.

---

[1] The Latin of this last sentence says something quite different: *Aspice si dominus ascendentis: aut mercurius dederunt vim saturno et ipse est in domo .8. significat hic natum mansurum in carcere et captivitate annis multis.* "See whether the lord of the Ascendant or Mercury has given power to Saturn, and Saturn is in the 8th house; this signifies that the native will remain in prison or captivity for many years." [RH] [Additional by MBE] It is possible to read 'Mercury' here, since its Hebrew name חמה כוכב (*Kohav ha'ma*) is often shortened to כוכב which also means a star in general, and at times is used for the planets as well. Therefore, the text can be read as: "Observe whether the rising sign, or Mercury in the rising sign, confers its power to Saturn in the fourth house."

[2] The preceding two conditions do not include a direct connection to the 12th house/or its ruler. These might be additional indicators for captivity, which is a signification of the 12 house. The 12th house is the Joy of Saturn and the subterranean 4th house, which signifies the end-of-the-matter, occasionally appears in statements about imprisonments. As for the 9th house, it is bad luck during travel.

[Enemies]

Abu [Ali][1] said: If the rising sign is Leo, most people will hate him, and that is true, for the Moon, which is the ruler of this house (the twelfth), indicates common people.[2]

If the rising sign is Virgo, one will have quarrels with kings and high [ranking] people; if Libra [is rising], one will have quarrels with the learned people; if Scorpio [is rising], most of the quarrels are with women; if Sagittarius [is rising], most of one's quarrels will be with men of war; if Capricorn or Aries [is rising], most of his quarrels will be with people of religion (or learning); if Aquarius [is rising], he will hate himself and will bring upon himself quarrels for no good reason; if Pisces [is rising], one will have quarrels with most of his friends; [52] if Taurus, [it will be] because of slander; and if Gemini, people will hate the native because of mean acts.

And this is the rule: If there are many planets in this house, one will have many enemies according to the nature of the planets.

[Domestic Animals]

Abu Mashar said that this house signifies animals that are used for man's riding, and I have already mentioned in *The Beginning of Wisdom* the kinds of animals that the planets indicate.

So observe if the ruler of the nativity is in this house, or beholds the ruler of the (this) house [in] an opposition aspect or a quartile aspect, then it indicates that [the native] will fall from the animal he will ride on. You will be able to know which animals are good for him when you observe the planet that beholds this house in a good aspect and has dominion over this place, and according to its species you will judge.

Mars is more harmful in this house than Saturn for it is Saturn's house of Joy and Mars' house of Gloom,[3] and it is the opposite for Saturn as it causes much harm in the sixth house for it is its house of Gloom, and not

---

[1] Latin has *Welius* as usual. RH

[2] When Leo is rising Cancer is in the 12th house, and the Moon, its ruler, is a significator of people in general. This kind of interpretation comes from the inherent relationship between the houses, which results from the overlay of the signs, regardless of the planets involved as detailed in the following text.

[3] By being opposite its house of Joy.

so [for] Mars, (in the sixth house) as it is its house of joy.[1]

THE ANNUAL REVOLUTIONS

[Computing the Annual Revolution Using the Day and Time of Birth][2]

The people of India say that the solar year is 365 days and $^1/_4$ [of a day] and $^1/_5$ of an hour, [and] therefore there are 93 degrees and 2 minutes between one annual revolution and another.[3]

---

[1] Note: This is the first time we have seen that the house opposite the "joy" of a planet is a house its sadness or gloom. It makes sense, but we have never seen it anywhere else. [RH]. [Additional by MBE] The Hebrew phrase is '*beit evlo*' (בית אבלו) 'the house of its mourning'. The idea is a condition opposite Joy, so I chose the word 'gloom'.

[2] The following discussion deals with the length of the solar year for the purpose of calculating the solar return chart. It is important to know the exact part of the day that is added to the whole number of 365 days since this gets translated into the arc of degrees by which the M.C. & Asc. of the solar return chart advance from one year to the next.

The length of the Tropical Year (defined as the interval between two successive passages of the sun through the Vernal Equinox) is 365.2422 mean solar days (365 days 5 hours 48 minutes and 46.08 seconds). 5h 48m 46.08s out of a day equals 87°11' 31.2" in the 360 wheel.

Ibn Ezra states that the number of degrees of arc that must be added to the M.C. of successive solar returns is 87°15', adding that it requires a long explanation, which he does not provide here. [RH]

[3] This is 365.258333 solar days or 365d 6h 12m 0s. This accords well with the modern value of the sidereal year of 365.25636d or 365d 6h 9m 9.5s. This confirms, if there was doubt in anyone's mind, that Indian astrology was using a sidereal zodiac in Ibn Ezra's time (12th century). Unfortunately we do not know which Indian authority Ibn Ezra is citing here.

In any case that would give an increment between solar returns of 93° 15' 17" of R.A.M.C (right ascension of the midheaven) difference, not 93° 02'. A brief explanation is in order concerning these numbers. The ancient and medieval method for computing solar returns consisted of adding the length of the year in days, hours, minutes and seconds to the original data of the chart for every elapsed year. This is a perfectly sound method as long as the length of the year is determined very accurately, otherwise the error is cumulative over the course of the years. They also determined that the R.A.M.C. advanced by a fixed amount every year depending on how much longer the year was than exactly 365.0 days.

70

The learned of Persia say that this is incremented by 1 minute in 115 years [literal alternative: the addition is one part of 115 in a day]. Thus, there are 93 degrees and 15 minutes between one revolution and another.[1]

Tabit [Ibn Qurra] said that the addition is 92 [degrees] and 24 minutes, and the addition of one part in a day is in 150 years.[2]

Ibrahim Azarkal says that the addition is one part in 160 years, and Abarcas said that they are 90 degrees with no addition or subtraction.

Ptolemy said that the [addition to the 365] year is less than $1/4$ of a day and a part of an hour and great Islamic scientists concurred with him like Ykh'ye Bin Abu Mantsur, and Almaradzi, and Ibn Al Makfa and Al Battani. And they agreed that the decrease (difference) is [53] one minute of a 106 in a day, so there are 86 degrees and 24 minutes between one annual revolution and another.[3]

There is no need to discuss these matters at length in order to know whether they are false or whether some of them are true. The truth is that most of them are correct, but require a long explanation.

The true [number] which has been tried and proven [going back] from today over two hundred years, and which has not been in error even by one minute [of a degree], is that there are 87 degrees and 15 minutes between one annual revolution and another.[4]

If we multiply the remainder given above, 0.258333d, by 360 we get 92° 59' 59.6". However this value is in solar days. To correct for the sidereal day (that is, 'sidereal' as in 'sidereal time' not 'sidereal' as in 'sidereal' year) which determines the advancement of the R.A.M.C. for each year, we must multiply that figure by 1.0027379,1 the ratio of the sidereal day to the solar day. This is gives us 93° 15' 16.2" which is a bit off from the value Ibn Ezra gives here. However, it must be pointed that numeric data is very often copied incorrectly, and we cannot assume that the data given here is what Ibn Ezra actually wrote. [RH]

[1] We cannot determine at this time what reference to 1 minute or part in 115 years means. However, the end result is much closer to the value of 93° 15' given in the previous note. This tells us that the Persians referred to here also used a sidereal zodiac. This confirms modern scholarship on this issue. [RH]

[2] It is also not clear what these values mean here and in the next paragraph. They are not precessional rates because the values of the years are clearly for sidereal years. [RH]

[3] Now we are dealing with various values of the tropical year. [RH]

[4] The proper value using modern data is 87° 25' 51" of R.A.M.C. per year. Ibn Ezra's value give us a tropical year value of 365.2417d as opposed to a modern value of 365.2422 an error or 43.2 seconds of time. I think that most modern readers would be surprised at how accurate these medieval values were.

[Step 1: Compute the Incremental Equatorial Degrees for the Ascendant]

Therefore, you have to observe how many years have passed for the native, and multiply the number by this increment (87° 15'). If the [resulting] addition is greater than [the number of] degrees of the wheel, subtract the degrees of the wheel (multiples of 360) and keep the remainder.

And [then] enter the mundane table [of houses] for the location of the nativity and take the steps (equatorial degrees)[1] you find for the [natal] rising degree and add to them that remainder.

[Step 2: Convert Equatorial Ascension Degrees to Ecliptical/Zodiacal Degrees]

Seek that result in the steps of the signs (equatorial degrees) in the mundane table, and take whatever you find against (corresponding to) this number in the even (equal) degrees of the wheel of the zodiac.

Then you will know the rising degree at the beginning of the year, and [from] the rising degree you can extract the uneven (temporal) hour.

[Step 3: Compute the Day of the Revolution in the Lunar Month]

And here I shall give you a calculation, so you can know in how many days of the lunar month the annual revolution of the native will be.

Know in how many days of the lunar month the native was born and

---

[RH]

[1] The Latin here uses forms of the word *passus* wherever the Hebrew has 'step'. *Passus* in Latin also means 'step'. Unfortunately so the does one of the common words for 'degree' which is *gradus*. Here is a possible solution to the terminological puzzle that this presents. In traditional astronomy there are two types of degrees. One is the usual geometric degree which is $^1/_{360}$th of a circle. There is also the time-degree which is $^1/_{360}$th of a diurnal rotation. It is measured in terms of the number of conventional equatorial degrees that pass over the Midheaven (R.A.M.C.) while some arc of the circle (such as a sign of the zodiac) is rising in the east or setting in the west. These are also referred to as "equatorial times." Perhaps this is what Ibn Ezra's use of the Hebrew word for 'step' and the Latin *passus* here indicates. When the Hebrew uses the word for 'degree', then it probably refers to normal degrees of arc or degrees upon the circle. [RH]

keep that [number].

Then multiply the number of whole years that have passed by 11, and add to the result the number [that you] kept, and extract multiples of 30, and the remainder that is less than 30 is the number of the days of the month in which the revolution occurs.[1]

[Step 4: Compute the Day of the Revolution in the Week][2]

If you wish to know what day in the week the revolution will occur, and which [temporal] hour it will be, [then] know [that] the day of the week when the native was born is the important thing, and what even (equal) hour it was, and make your calculation from the beginning of the day or from the beginning of the night.

Then multiply the number of whole years that have passed by 1 day and 5 hours and 49 minutes, [and keep in mind] that every hour has sixty minutes, [54] and make (convert) the minutes into hours and from the hours [make] days and add it all up, and if the result is greater than 7 [days] discard all [multiples of] 7 that are contained in them, and add the remainder that is less than 7 as well as the hours and the minutes, to the whole days in the week that have passed for the native, and add the hours to the [natal equal] hours and the minutes to the [natal equal] minutes, and then you will know the moment of the revolution.

[Step 5: Compute the Temporal Hour of the Revolution]

You can convert the even (equal) hour to an uneven (temporal) hour as is written in the book of tables.

[Example]

And I shall give you an example. Let us assume that the native was born

---

[1] The above computation and its purpose are unclear. It seems to use an average length of 30 days for the Hebrew calendar month. The Hebrew calendar month alternates between 29 or 30 days, with a leap month every four years. A simple test of this formula did not bear it out. Also, to the best of my knowledge, the date in the Hebrew month does not have any traditional astrological meaning, and does not appear as such in any of the other texts by Ibn Ezra.

[2] In order to find the Planetary Ruler of the Day, to be followed later by Planetary Ruler of the (temporal) Hour.

on a Tuesday on the 9th of the month, whatever month it may be, at 2 even (equal) hours and 35 minutes that have passed of the day. And let us assume that 10 whole years have passed for the native. And we wish to know on what day of the month the revolution will be.

So we multiply 10 by 11 and get 110, and we add to that 9 days that have passed of the month at the time of the nativity, and the result is 119. We discard multiples of 30 and 29 remain, thus the revolution is near the end of the month.

We want to know the day of the week and the hour and the minute, [so] we multiply the 10 years we have by 1 day and the result is 10 days, and we multiply the [5] hours by 10 and we get 50 hours. We make of these [hours] 2 days and add them to those [10] above and so they are 12 days [and] 2 hours remain. We also multiply the [49] minutes by 10 and we get 490, [which] we divide by 60 and we get 8 hours.

We add them to those [2 AM of birth] above and the result is 10 [hours]. There remain 10 minutes which we add to the number of hours that passed from the beginning of the day on Tuesday at the time of birth (2 whole hours), resulting in 12 hours, and [we] also [add] the [10] minutes that we have [as the remainder] to the minute[s] of the hour of birth (0:35) resulting in 45, which is ³/₄ of an hour.

We discard 7 from the days we have and what remains is 5 days and 12 hours and 45 minutes.

We start counting from the beginning of Tuesday. From the time of sunrise on Tuesday until it rises on Wednesday it is one day, and [so] the [additional 5] days are completed at sunrise [55] on Sunday.

From the remaining [12] hours we shall make an arc by taking for each hour 15 degrees, and we take ¹/₄ from the [remaining] minutes (i.e., divide the minutes by 4) and that will be degrees, and if 1 [minute of time] remains after the division by 4 we shall take 15 minutes [of a degree], and if 2 [remain we shall take] 30 [minutes], and if 3 [remain we shall take] 45 minutes, and this arc is the distance from the rising sign at the moment of birth (in equal degrees).

Add these degrees to the steps (equal degrees) that you find for the rising degree in the mundane table, and seek the resulting number in the mundane table, and take what is [listed] for this number in the wheel of the zodiac, and this way comes out equal to the addition of 87 [degrees and] 15 [minutes] for each year, as I have mentioned [above].

You can know whether this calculation comes out by day or by night[by taking the arc of the day, as written in the *Book of Tables*, and subtract from it the distance between the steps (equal degrees) for the degree of the Sun which are called oriental, and the steps (equal degrees) [that you have] for the rising degree (of the revolution), and the result is the remaining arc of the day.

If this remainder is greater than the arc of the hours that you have, subtract the arc from it, and divide the remainder by the arc of the uneven hour. Whatever results in hour[s] and the part of an hour, subtract from twelve hours, and then you will find the hour of the revolution and its minute which is on Sunday.

If the arc of the hours that you have is greater than the remaining arc of the day, subtract the remaining arc from the arc of hours that you have and divide the result by the arc of the uneven (temporal) hours of the night, and then you will find how many uneven hours and minutes of an hour passed from the night of Monday. And always do it according to this example.

[Evaluation of the Annual Revolution – Important Considerations]

[The first thing to observe:] You have to observe every year for many things, and they are twelve: and I will first mention to you the most important of them all. Know which is the [natal] place of life that indicates the life of the native [56] as written in [the chapter on] the First House, and direct it by the two [methods of] directions, as I have mentioned in *The Book of Reasons.*[1]

If you find a planet or its aspect at the degree where the direction has reached, [then] assign all the power to that planet, and it will serve the number of years according to its light, as written in the book *The Beginning of Wisdom* and the ruler of the bound participates with it.

If there is no planet there, nor its aspect, [then] the ruler of the bound will be the indicator of good or bad, and include with it the ruler of the house.[2] You ought to observe the ruler of the bound [by noting] its strength in the nativity and how strong it is in every annual revolution, throughout all the time that it indicates (governs); for if it is strong in the nativity and weak in the [annual] revolution, it will harm but little, and if it is weak in the nativity and strong in the [annual] revolution, it will do

---

[1] This appears to refer to the primary direction of the Ascendant to significators and through the bounds. [RH]

[2] The Latin here is garbled. The Hebrew appears to have it correct. [RH]

little good, and if strong in both times, it will add good upon good, and if weak in both, it is the opposite; this is the first thing you should observe.

The second [thing to observe] is the ruler of the triplicity according to its years, as it [also] indicates (governs) the years that are at the time of the [annual] revolution. If [the native is] in the first one-third of his life, it is indicated (governed) by the first ruler of the triplicity of the place of life, and the two others (triplicity rulers) at the other times. And observe this planet [to see] how it is in the nativity and in the [annual] revolution.

The third [thing to observe] is that you should observe the years according to Ptolemy, beginning from the Moon and ending with Saturn.[1] And according to the influence of that planet in the nativity and in the [annual] revolution so you will judge.

The fourth [thing to observe] is the division called Al Firdar. And you should know that [for] one born by day the Sun indicates (governs) the native for [the first] ten years, and it alone [rules] in the [first] one-seventh of the number, and the other planets will participate with it in its remaining six sevenths.

And [then] Venus begins and then Mercury, accordingly. So if the Sun in the nativity is in a conjunction with Saturn or Mars, or in a bad aspect with them, sickness will befall the native during the time when that planet that harms the Sun will participate with it (during its sub-period).[2] It is worse if one of them is the ruler of the sixth house. [57]

Then Venus will indicate alone in the [first] one-seventh of its share, all of which is eight years, and then the others will participate with it. So if Venus in the nativity is in a bad aspect with Mars, the native will come to shame and great sorrow because of a woman in the time when Mars participates with Venus.

After Venus Mercury will indicate alone in the [first] one seventh of its share, which is thirteen years, and then the others will participate with it. When Saturn participates with it, it will indicate serious illness, especially if Mercury is the ruler of the nativity.[3]

---

[1] Ptolemy's Ages of Life (Ashmand, 138-139).

[2] This refers to the fact that in the firdar there are always two rulers, the long period ruler and the several sub-rulers of the one-sevenths of the long period. If a planet is afflicted, then the difficulty signified by that affliction will come to pass in the afflicted planet's period during the subperiod ruled by the afflicting planet. [RH]

[3] If Gemini or Virgo is rising, then Saturn rules the 8th house or the 6th house respectively.

After that the Moon will be alone [as the ruler] in the [first] one-seventh of its share, which is nine years, and in the other [six] sevenths the others will participate with her. When Saturn participates with her it will indicate fear and sickness [that comes] from cold.

After her Saturn will be the indicator alone in [the first] one-seventh of its share, which is eleven years, and when it [rules] alone by itself it will indicate quarrels that befall the native and having evil thoughts, [but] when Jupiter participates with him it will remove this harm.

After him, Jupiter will be the indicator alone in [the first] one-seventh of its share, and it will indicate good [things] in this one-seventh of its share which is twelve years, and the others will participate with it after that.

After that Mars will be the indicator alone in [the first] one-seventh of its share, which is seven years.

And then the one indicating alone for three years is the North Node, and after that the South Node [for] two years.

The total of the years is seventy five; so if the years of the native are longer than this number, the planets will return [in this sequence], beginning from the Sun.

If the nativity is by night, the Moon begins at night according to the number of its share, and after her Saturn, until the last planet Mercury, and then the North Node, and ending with the South Node.[1]

Astrologers have discussed every one of these at length, and I shall give you two rules. One rule is that you should observe whether the planet

---

[1] Note the disagreement here with Al-Qabisi (Alcabitius) and Bonatti who seem to place the nodal periods between those or Mars and the Sun whether by day or by night. Al-Qabisi and Bonatti (who explicitly follows Al-Qabisi) are the only sources for this alternate procedure and it is not certain that that is what even they had in mind. Both texts are ambiguous on this point. In his section on the *fardāñyah* (what Ibn Ezra calls Al Firdar) Al-Qabisi gives the usual sequence for day births just as Ibn Ezra does. However, when he comes to the nocturnal sequence, he says the following:

When the birth is by night, begin the governance from the Moon. It governs the years of its *fardāñyah*, which are nine years. Likewise planet after planet, as we have described in the section on the Sun. (Al-Qabisi, 135-137)

It is not specified what one is supposed to do with the periods of the nodes and so it is also not clear that he explicitly intended the node periods to be placed after the period of Mars and before that of the Sun in the nocturnal sequence.[RH]

77

is strong in the nativity or weak; for if it is strong, it will indicate good even if it is a malefic planet, and when it is weak, even [58] if it's a benefic planet, it will be of little use when the time comes for it to be the indicator.

The second rule is that you should look by way of nature; for if the nativity is by day, when it's time for Venus to participate with the Sun it will not indicate that [the native] will take a new wife or enjoy women for his nature is not appropriate [for this yet];[1] but we will judge, if Venus is in a good place [in the nativity], that women will love him at that time. If the nativity is by night, the Sun will be the indicator after two-thirds of one's life, [and] then it will indicate pleasure with women. And this concludes the fourth [thing to look for in the annual revolution].

---

[1] This is because for diurnal births the firdar of Venus takes place in childhood. [RH]

[Profection]

The fifth [thing to observe] is the end sign, and that is always [counted] in even degrees (zodiacal). And so you will do. In the first year the end sign is from the beginning of the rising degree [counting] 30 degrees until the next sign [and so on]. And look to see if there is a benefic planet there in the nativity, [for] it indicates good for him that year, [. . .[1] . . .] and if a malefic planet [is there], it is the opposite, as it will bring him illness or harm according to its place; for if it is in the sixth house, it indicates illness, if in the eighth, [it will indicate] fear for life, if in the second, [it will indicate] loss of money, if in the fifth, [it will indicate] worry concerning children, and likewise for all the houses according to what they signify. And if in the [annual] revolutions there is a benefic planet in the end sign, it indicates good that will come to the native that has not been anticipated, and if [an] evil [planet, then it is] the opposite.[2]

And you must include the ruler of the sign with it for this is an important principle.

The sixth [thing to observe] is the end sign from the place of life, [counted] in even degrees up to thirty (for one year). So you will do every year until the end of twelve years which is the number of the signs, and this (twelve year cycle) is repeated until his death.

The seventh [thing to look for] is that you should observe the ruler of the [planetary] hour of the nativity, which is always an uneven hour. In the first year that [planet] will be the indicator, and the second is [ruled by]

---

[1] At this point in the sentence there is a short phrase which does not make any sense, neither by itself, nor in the context. It reads: ". . . זה קודם ידוע מדבר אם . . ." ('*im midavar yadua kodem ze*') and translates as: "whether from a matter known before that." I chose to omit it since it does not appear to have a significant astrological meaning as such, and the meaning of the rest of the text is not affected by its omission. [Additional by RH] The Latin has the same thing as the Hebrew.

[2] The text is not entirely clear and can be understood in two ways. One is to observe whether the Profected natal sign contains a benefic/malefic planet in the Solar Return anywhere in the chart, which is practically the same as observing a regular transit to that sign/house in the natal chart. The other is to assume some text corruption, and read it to mean, paraphrased by me: "If the natal Profected sign for the year, or its ruler, or the planet found in it, are strong (angular, in dignity, etc.) in the Solar Return, their effect will be noticeable, especially if strong/good both in the natal and the Solar Return charts." The latter interpretation is more like the standard astrological principle that always evaluates current astrological effects in the context of the natal chart.

79

the planet that is under it in the spheres according to the sequence of Sun, Venus, Mercury, Moon, Saturn, Jupiter, Mars. And according to its influence in the nativity and the annual revolution so will be the year.

The eighth [thing to observe] is the ruler of the rising sign for it [59] indicates the first year, and the planet that is under it indicates the second year, and so until seven years.

[The ninth thing to look for¹] is the opinion of Enoch that the ruler of the hour of the nativity serves in the first year in the first house which is the house of life, and in the second year the house of wealth (second house), and so until the end of twelve years, and then its repeated again and again.

The tenth [thing to consider] is the annual revolution [itself], as you ought to observe the rising degree at the moment of the revolution, as I have explained, and the ruler of the rising sign, and the planet that you find in it at the annual revolution.

The eleventh [principle] is that you should observe which planet in the annual revolution returns to its place in the nativity, for it will bring about whatever it indicates according to its nature and the houses over which it has dominion.

The twelfth [thing to observe] is when one of the planets at the moment of the revolution is in the place of another planet at the moment of the nativity, and I shall give you a rule. If you find a benefic planet in the annual revolution in a place where a malefic is in the nativity, it indicates that it will remove the harm of the malefic and will bring good for the native. It is the opposite if you find a malefic planet in the annual revolution in a place where a benefic was at the time of the nativity; if the malefic in the annual revolution is in a place where a malefic was at the time of the nativity, then it adds adversity upon adversity, and a benefic in place of a benefic will add good upon good.

THE MONTHS

[Sub-Division into Months in the Profected Year]

---

¹ The text does not explicitly list this item as a separate ninth point in the evaluation process. However, it is followed directly by number ten, with nine seemingly missing. The contents is sufficiently different from the previous point, so it is plausible to consider this as the ninth item.

Observe in the nativity the place of the planets and the Lot of Fortune, and assign to each month a sign, and begin counting from the rising degree up to 30 degrees for 30 days and 10 hours. The month that arrives at a benefic planet will indicate good, and the opposite if it arrives at a malefic [planet].[1]

Enoch said that when the end-sign (the profection) is [in] the first house, or the fifth or the seventh or the ninth or the tenth or the eleventh, it is an indication of a good year, except when there is a malefic in [any of] these places.[2]

If you wish to know the months during the annual revolution, begin from the end sign (the profected place) and give every month 2½ degrees. The end of the month is when [60] the sun reaches the next sign, at the [same] number of degrees and minutes where it was [in its natal] sign. Thus, every degree gets twelve days and approximately one sixth of a day.[3]

Consider the aspects of the planets at the moment of the nativity as well as in the annual revolution to the end-house, and direct in this way the degrees to the place of the conjunction of the planets, or to their aspect, and from this way you can know what will happen to the native day by day. And include with this the rising sign at the moment of birth and the rising [sign] in the annual revolution.[4]

---

[1] This system simply moves the profected points by 30 degrees for every $^1/_{12}$th of the year. The year is 365.24220 days and $^1/_{12}$th of this is 30 days plus 10h 29m 38s. This is not the system of monthly profections advocated by Ptolemy as is shown below. [RH]

[2] This paragraph appears to be a throwback to the annual profection and seems to have nothing to do with monthly profections except insofar as the same principles apply to these as to annual profections. [RH]

[3] This entire section on months is about all techniques that are designed to elicit the month of an effect from profections. Here Ibn Ezra is showing how to get the month out of the annual profections. Annual profections move at the rate of 30° per year. Therefore they move at the rate of 2.5° per month and he explicitly defines the month as the time it takes the transiting Sun to move through 30° of the zodiac. So for every 30° the transiting Sun has moved since the solar return, the annually profected positions move 2.5°. [RH]

[4] The Latin has: *Et considera ascriptum stellarum hora natitivitatis. Et iterum in revolutione* [text has *irrevolutione*] *anni in domo finis: et ducas ista via gradus ad locum coniunctionis* [text has *coniectionis* which does not make sense in this context] *planetarum: aut ad eorum aspectus: et isto modo poteris scire omne*

Ptolemy said that we should assign 30 degrees of the end-house to 28 days and 2 hours and direct the degrees in this way until the end-house returns a second time at the end of the year. The astrologers that came after him agreed with this way.[1]

He also said that in the annual revolution we should give to every 1¼ degree 1 day[2] and that this direction should be in the steps of the sign in the mundane table. It is also a proven thing [in order] to know what happens day by day when the Sun moves one whole degree from its place, whether it traverses the degree in [exactly] one day, or in fewer or more hours.

And you should give to 1 day 12 degrees, [starting] from three places. One is the rising degree at the moment of the nativity; two, from the degree of the end-house; and three, from the rising sign at the annual revolution.[3]

And this, that I have told you, you should do in the two ways; [one], in even degrees of the wheel of the zodiac, and [two] in the steps of the signs in the mundane table (equatorial degrees). And so you will do month by month until the end of the year.

---

futurum quolibet die. Et huic adiunge signum ascendens hora nativititatis. Et itidem ascendens in revolutione anni. "Consider the attribution of the stars at the time of the nativity, and again in the revolution of the year in the house of the ending [profection], and you should direct the degrees in this manner to the place of the conjunction of the planets or their aspects; and in this manner you will be able to know everything that will be for each day. And to this join the rising sign at the time of the nativity and likewise the Ascendant in the revolution of the year." [RH]

[1] This is the Ptolemaic method of computing monthly profections. His logic is simple. The monthly profected positions of each point should coincide with the annually profected positions of each point at the moment of the solar return. Since the annual profections move at the rate of one sign per year, the monthly profections have to move 13 signs a year (12 to go around plus 1 to catch up with the annuals). The year divided by 13 gives 28d 2h 17m 36s. This is origin of Ptolemy's value. [RH]

[2] The Latin has ¼ degree not 1 and ¼ degree per day. But this does not make sense either way. [RH]

[3] This is a daily profection which results in a complete revolution of the profected positions in 30 days. This is the diurnal equivalent of Ibn Ezra's monthly profection as given above gving 2 and ½ days per sign, whereas Ptolemy's daily profection gives 2 ⅓ days per sign. [RH]

THE DAYS

[Planetary Days and Hours][1]

Observe in the nativity which planet is in a good place; the day of that[2] planet is good for the native; every planet which is combust, or in its house of fall, or in the sixth house, or in the twelfth house, the day of that planet is bad for him. The power of that planet will be more noticeable if it is the ruler of the nativity whether good or bad. In the same way [judge] the nights, and also the the uneven (temporal) hours in the day and in the night, and the reason is that they are always divided by 12. [61]

THE GOOD SIGNS

[A Brief Discussion on Elections]

[For] the inception of everything [observe] the [sign of] first house, but make sure that it is not above the earth by more than 5 degrees, for then it is in the influence of the twelfth [house], and then [observe] the tenth house, and then the eleventh, and then the fifth house. The second house and the fourth are [of] medium [strength], and so are the ninth and the third. Only the eighth and the sixth and the twelfth are bad.[3]

You should know the election that the native seeks; for if he wants to drink medicine, make his [natal] rising sign [to be the rising sign of the

---

[1] This section refers to the traditional scheme of planetary rulership for the day of the week and for the temporal, (uneven) hours. The hours are based on dividing the total time of daylight divided by 12, and the same for the night time, for any day in the year. The sequence of rulership is: The Sun rules the daytime of Sunday and its first temporal hour. In the same way, the Moon rules Monday and its first temporal hour, and in this manner Mars rules Tuesday, Mercury rules Wednesday, Jupiter rules Thursday, Venus rules Friday and Saturn rules Saturday.

[2] Latin omits "the day of . . ." [RH]

[3] A variant text from PAR1056, after the first house: ". . . and after that the tenth house then the eleventh house then the 5th house and the fourth house and the seventh. The second house and the eighth are middling and so are the ninth and the third. Only the sixth and the twelfth are bad." This a known scheme, and the presence of the eighth house is because it is one of the adjacent houses , located next to the pivots, and therefore considered strong. Yet, strong does not make it good.

elected chart], and if [he wants] to increase wealth, [take] the second house [of the nativity], and if [he wishes] to go to a high-ranking person, choose for him the [natal] tenth house.

If there is one of the benefic planets in one of these good houses, and you can make its degree the rising degree [in the election chart], then he will have much benefit, and if you must use one of these [natal] houses, and one of the malefics was there, be careful not use the [exact] place of the malefic; move away from its place to the end of its [orb of] light, as in this example where the tenth house is 4 degrees of Gemini and Saturn is at 12 degrees [of Gemini]. It is known that its body's [orb of] light is 9 degrees, which reaches 21 degrees of Gemini (when added to the place of Saturn); [therefore] assign the ascendant (of the election) from 22 degrees and up.

THE DIRECTIONS

[The Geographical Direction to Consider in Elections]

Observe the place of the benefics and malefics [to see] in which quadrant they are, as explained in the book *The Beginning of Wisdom*, and choose for him to go in the direction where the benefic planets are.

THE COUNTRIES

[Relocation Considerations]

Every country whose sign[1] coincides with a [place of] a malefic at the moment of the nativity is bad for the native; so choose for him to reside in a place of the benefics.

THE COLORS

The colors of the garment that is good for the native you will know from

---

[1] Signs were allocated to countries using a variety of schemes, not all of which involved rising signs. See Ptolemy, Book II, chapter III (Ashmand, 43-52). RH]

the color that is indicated by the ruler of the nativity, and that is the planet that has [the most] dominion in the five places of life. And if it is in a conjunction or an aspect with a planet superior to it, that superior planet which receives the power will be the ruler of the nativity,[1] and you should mix the nature of both according to their place vis-a-vis the Sun, the sign they are in and the pivots.

---

[1] This is an interesting addition to the formula of the Almuten.

[The following is a free form translation of the rhymed colophon, apparently added here by the copyist of this text, dating his work. The Jewish year matches the information from the Vatican Library. The month seems to refer to *Av*, the month of lamentations (about August), which is historical time of mourning for the destruction of the First and the Second Temple in Jerusalem.]

The One of Awful Praise who does great things, has helped to complete [these] nativities and signs in the year 1436, [in the] the month that fell [from the grace of] God and on Saturday of '*Menahem*' I shall begin to write The Book of Lights.

נורא תהלות עושה גדלות עזר לכלות מולדי מזלות
בשנת הקצ"ו ירח אשר מט עם אל ונשמט מבית
מסילות ובש מנחם אחל לתחם ספר מאורות

APPENDIX A: IBN EZRA'S ASTROLOGICAL WORKS

1) *The Beginning of Wisdom (Re'shit Ho'khmah)*: This is Ibn Ezra's best known astrological text, encompassing the fundamental components of the astrological doctrine.

2) *The Book of Reasons (Se'fer Ha'Te'amim)*: Commentary and additional material for all the topics in *The Beginning Of Wisdom*.

3) *The Book of Nativities (Se'fer Ha'Moladot)*: An expanded discussion on the astrological houses in the birth chart, on chart rectification, as well as a section on prognostication - the annual revolutions and other astrological cycles.

4) *The Book of Lights (Se'fer Ha'Me'orot)*: Medical astrology, based on the Sun and the Moon and their condition in the decumbiture chart.

5) *The Book of Elections (Se'fer Ha'Miv'harim)*: Electional Astrology – affecting a desirable outcome by electing a good time to begin an endeavor.

6) *The Book of Questions (Se'fer Ha'She'elot)*: Horary astrology – finding an answer to a pressing question.

7) *The Book of the World (Se'fer Ha'Olam)*: Mundane astrology – the celestial influences in the world – non-personal astrology.

8) *Predictions Made In the Year 1154 (He'zionot Rabbi Avraham Ibn Ezra She'haza Al Sh'nat 4914 La'Ye'tsira)*: Mundane astrology. A very short treatise containing mundane forecast based on the great Conjunction of Jupiter-Saturn in Capricorn, which was coming up in 1166.

9) *Horoscope Analysis for a Newborn (Mishpatei Ha'Nolad)*: An example of chart analysis based on birth data that seems to fit October 14-15, 1160, at Narbonne, France.

10) *The Treatise of the Astrolabe (Kli Ha'Ne'hoshet)*: Includes computation of the 12 houses of the horoscope, how to determine the astrological aspects, Fixed Stars of the First and the Second

Magnitude, their names and description, computing their Precession rate in the Tropical Zodiac.

11) Muhammad bin Almatani's Explanations For *The Astronomical Tables of Muhammad al-Khwarizmi* (*Ta'amei Lu'hot al-Khwarizmi*): A translation from Arabic into Hebrew and an Introduction by Ibn Ezra. Contains an interesting account of the introduction of Hindu astronomical calculations into Islam. Comparison to Ptolemy's *Almagest*. Discussion of the Precession regarding the position of the Fixed Stars.

12) A *Book by Mashallah on the Eclipses of the Sun and the Moon:* Ibn Ezra's translation from Arabic into Hebrew. Mundane astrology: Weather – judged from the Aries Ingress, eclipses, and the planetary conjunctions.

Astrological and Astronomical Terms Found in *Moladot*:

The list contain terms that are specific to astronomy and astrology, as well
as phrases and words that may also be used in ordinary language for other
purposes. Some of these words have more than one astrological meaning
and must be understood in the context. The terms are grouped and
sequenced by topics. Under Transliteration, the characters 'kh' are
pronounced as the 'ch' in Scottish 'loch'.

His Astrological Work

Translation	Terms & Expressions	Transliteration
GENERAL		
Astrolabe. Literally, a copper instrument.	כלי נחשת	Klei Nekhoshet
The native. The new-born.	הנולד	*Nolad*
Nativity – the birth chart.	מולד	*Molad*
Computation, reckoning. Literally, fixing, mending. In older Hebrew, making.	תיקון	*Tikkun*
Equation. Literally, scales.	מאזנים	*Mozna'im*
The method of multiplication, also of proportion.	דרך הערך	*Derekh ha'e'rekh*
Multiply (the imperative)	ערוך	*A'rokh*
An example. Literally, similarity, imagination, an imagined image.	דמיון	*Dimyon*
THE WHEEL		
Wheel	גלגל	*Galgal*
Degree	מעלה	*Ma'a'la*
Minute. Literally, part.	חלק	*Khe'lek*
The solid wheel, the auge. The orbit of a planet.	גלגל המוצק	*Galgal ha'mu'tzak*
The planet's elevation in the small wheel (the epicycle).	מקום גבהות הגלגל הקטן	*Mekom gavhut hagalgal hakatan*
The planet's lowest position (in the wheel).	מקום שפלותו	*Me'kom shifluto*

The equator. Literally, the straight or even wheel.	גלגל היושר	Galgal ha'yosher
The zodiac. Literally, the wheel of the signs.	גלגל המזלות	Galgal ha'mazalot
The ecliptic. Literally, the computation of the engirdling wheel.	חשב אפודת הגלגל	Kheshev afudat ha'galgal
Even degrees (in the zodiac). Literally, even or straight degrees.	מעלות ישרות	Ma'a lot yesharot
Equatorial degrees. Literally, degrees of the steps of the earth.	מעלות מצעדי הארץ	Ma'a lot mitz'adei ha'a'retz
The mundane table (rising and culminating signs and degrees per location)	לוח הארץ	Lu'akh ha'a'retz
Long 'steps', for signs or degrees taking longer than the average time to ascend.	מצעדים ארוכים	Mitz'adim a'rukim
Short 'steps', for signs or degrees (taking shorter than the average time to ascend)	מצעדים קצרים	Mitz'adim ktzarim
The arc of the day, the diurnal arc.	קשת היום	Keshet ha'yom
A temporal hour. Literally, a crooked hour. Uneven.	שעה מעוותת	Sha'a me'u've'tet
An equatorial hour. Literally, even or straight hour.	שעה ישרה	Sha'a ye'shara
Latitude (either geographical or ecliptical).	מרחב	Merkhav
Side.	פאה	Pe'a
South side.	פאת דרום	Pe'at darom
Southern.	דרומי	Dromi
North side.	פאת צפון	Pe'at tzafon
Northern.	צפוני	Tzfoni
Terrestrial latitude.	מרחב הארץ	Merkhav ha'a'retz
Oriental.	מזרחי	Mizrakhi
Occidental.	מערבי	Ma'aravi

THE MUNDANE WHEEL

The quadrant in the mundane wheel	רביע הגלגל	Ravi'a ha'galgal
House. Used both for houses in the mundane wheel and for the zodiacal domiciles of the planets.	בית	Ba'it
Division of the houses	חלוק הבתים	Khiluk ha'batim
Computed according to the geographical latitude (pertains to the houses)	מתוקנים כפי מרחב הארץ	Me'tukanim kefi merkhav ha'a'retz
Pivot. Pole. Used for the four angular houses.	יתד	Ya'ted
The rising degree in the east, the ascendant. Literally, the growing or sprouting degree.	המעלה הצומחת	Ha'ma'ala ha'tzomakhat
The rising sign.	המזל הצומח	Hamazal hatsome'akh
The midheaven. Literally, the line of the middle or half the heaven.	קו חצי השמים	Kav khatzi ha'sha'ma'im
The midheaven. Literally, 'the upper pivot'.	יתד הרום	Ya'ted ha'rom
The angle of the lower heaven. Literally, the pivot of the abyss.	יתד התהום	Ya'ted ha'tehom
The setting degree, the descendant.	המעלה השוקעת	Ha'ma'ala ha'shoka'at
The succedent houses (next to the pivots or angular house). Literally, the adjacent houses.	הבתים הסמוכים	Ha'batim ha'smukhim
The cadent, falling houses.	הבתים הנופלים	Ha'batim ha'noflim

The Signs

English	Hebrew	Transliteration
Form or shape. Also used to denote constellational images.	צורה	*Tzura*
1. Zodiacal sign. Literally, luck. 2. A general term for a chart configuration.	מזל	*Mazal*
1. Nature (characteristic or quality). 2. Element (fire, earth, air, water).	תולדת	*Toledet*
Triplicity (synonym for the elements).	שלישות	*Shalishut*
The fire element. Literally, of the nature of fire.	תולדת האש	*Toledet ha'esh*
The earth element. Literally, of the nature of earth.	תולדת העפר	*Toledet he'afar*
The air element. Literally, of the nature of air.	תולדת האייר	*Toledet ha'avir*
The water element. Literally, of the nature of water.	תולדת המים	*Toledet ha'ma'im*
1. Bound (an uneven subdivision of the sign). Also known as term. Literally, boundary. 2. Climata, a range of geographical latitude.	גבול	*Gevul*
Face (a one-third subdivision of the sign). Literally, face.	פנים	*Pa'nim*
Exaltation (of planets in certain signs). Literally, honor, dignity.	כבוד	*Ka'vod*
House of Exaltation. Literally, its house of honor.	בית כבודו	*Beit kevodo*

English	Hebrew	Transliteration
House of Detriment. Literally, its house of hate.	בית שנאתו	Beit sin'a'to
House of Fall. Literally, its house of disgrace.	בית קלונו	Beit klono
House of Joy.	בית שמחתו	Beit simkhato
House of Gloom. Literally, its house of mourning.	בית אבלו	Beit evlo
Changeable or movable sign.	מזל מתהפך	Mazal mit'ha'pekh
Signs of long ascension. Literally, long signs.	מזלות ארוכים	Mazalot a'ru'kim
Signs of short ascension. Literally, short sign.	מזלות קצרים	Mazalot ktzarim
The Lot of Fortune. Same literally. 'Goral' is used for 'fate or destiny', but also for 'lot' as in 'luck or chance'.	הגורל הטוב	Ha'goral ha'tov

PLANETS' CLASSIFICATION

English	Hebrew	Transliteration
Planet. Literally, servant, attendant.	משרת	Mesharet
A malefic planet (Mars & Saturn). Literally, a harmful star.	כוכב מזיק	Kokhav ma'zik
A benefic planet (Venus & Jupiter). Literally, a good star.	כוכב טוב	Kokhav tov
The inferior planets (Mercury & Venus).	הכוכבים השפלים	Ha'kokhavim ha'shfalim
The superior planets (Mars, Jupiter and Saturn).	הכוכבים העליונים	Ha'kokhavim ha'elionim

PLANETARY INFLUENCE

English	Hebrew	Transliteration
Ruler. The one that has dominion.	שליט	Shalit
The house ruler (through the sign on the cusp). Literally, the house owner, the landlord.	בעל הבית	Ba'al ha'ba'it

1. Dominion, government. 2. Rulership. For both, governing chart placements.	ממשלה שלטון	Memshala Shilton
The ruler of the Face (a sub-division of the sign).	שר הפנים	Sar ha'panim
Strength, or influence, depending on the context.	כח	Ko'akh
Under the influence of, or under the power of.	בכח	Be'ko'akh
Mixture (of different qualities), or Nature of . . .	ממסך	Mimsakh

PLANETARY ASPECTS

Aspect. Literally, a look, a glance.	מבט	Mabat
Aspecting. Literally, looking.	מביט	Mabit
1. Conjunction 2. The New Moon before birth.	מחברת המחברת	Makhberet
A harmonious aspect (trine or sextile). Literally, love or friendship aspect.	מבט אהבה	Mabat a'ha'va
A hostile aspect (square or opposition)	מבט איבה	Mabat ei'va
A sextile aspect	מבט ששית	Mabat shishit
A trine aspect.	מבט שלישית	Mabat shlishit
A quartile aspect.	מבט רביעית	Mabat revi'it
An opposition aspect.	מבט נכח	Mabat nokhakh
1. Opposition (be on the opposite side). 2. The Full Moon. 3. The Full Moon before birth.	נכח הנכח	Nokhakh Ha'nokhakh
The orb of its light (the orb of influence). Literally, the light of its body.	אור גופו	Or gu'fo

PLANETARY CONDITIONS AND PHASES WITH REGARD TO THE SUN		
Retrograde. Literally, going backward.	שב אחורנית	Shav a'khoranit
Combust.	נשרף	Nisraf
Under the light of the Sun (within a prescribed orb).	תחת אור השמש	Takhat or ha'shemesh
Its phase with the Sun. Literally, its proportion...	ערכו אל השמש	Erko el ha'shemesh
Oriental of the Sun.	מזרחי מן השמש	Mizrakhi min ha'shemesh
Occidental of the Sun.	מערבי מן השמש	Ma'a'ravi min ha'shemesh
The first Quadrant with regard to the Sun. Literally, . . . on the side of the Sun.	הרביעית הראשונה מפאת השמש	Ha'revi'it ha'rishona mi'pe'at ha'shemesh
1. Station (of planets). 2. The period of the station, first (retrograde) or second (direct). 3. A period, a term, as in pregnancy.	מעמד	Ma'a'mad

TIMING & LIFE		
The measure of life.	מדת החיים	Midat ha'khai'im
The Hyleg. Literally, The Place of Life.	מקום החיים	Mekom ha'kai'im
Place of abscission. Literally, a place of cutting off.	מקום כרת	Mekom ka'ret
The abscissor. The one that cuts off.	הכורת	Ha'ko'ret
To direct (symbolically progressing a planet from one place to another). Literally, to drive, to direct.	לנהג	Le'na'heg
Directions (of planets, as above).	ניהוגים	Ni'hu'gim

1. Period. 2. The annual revolution of the sun.	תְּקוּפָה	*Tequfa*
The annual revolution for the world, the Aries Ingress at the Vernal Equinox. Literally, the period of the world.	תְּקוּפַת הָעוֹלָם	*Tqufat ha'olam*

BIBLIOGRAPHY & REFERENCES

Al-Biruni. *The Book of Instruction in the Elements of the Art of Astrology*. Translated by R. Ramsey Wright. London: Luzac and Co., 1934.

Ben Menahem, Naphtali, ed. "Introduction" in *Sefer Ha-Te'amim* (*The Book of Reasons*). Jerusalem: Mosad Harav Kook, 1941. (Hebrew)

Dorotheus of Sidon. *Carmen Astrologicum*, ed. David Pingree. Leipzig: Teubner, 1976.

Epstein, Meira B. "Avraham Ibn Ezra – His Life and his Work." In *The Astrology Book – The Encyclopedia of Heavenly Influences*, edited by James R. Lewis (2nd Edition), 349-356. USA: Visible Ink Press, 2003.

Ibn Ezra, Avraham. *The Book of Reasons,* translated by Meira B. Epstein. (www.Bear-Star.com, 1994)

_____. *The Beginning of Wisdom*. Translated by Meira Epstein. Reston, VA: ARHAT Publications, 1998.

_____. *The Beginning of Wisdom; an Astrological Treatise by Abraham Ibn Ezra*. Edited and translated by Raphael Levy and Francisco Cantera. Baltimore, MD: Johns Hopkins Press, 1939. (See introduction by Raphael Levy.)

Fleischer, Yehuda Leib. "Introduction" in *Sefer Ha'Olam* (*The Book of The World*). Timishurara, Romania: 1937 (Hebrew)

Fleischer, Yehuda Leib. "Introduction" in *Sefer Ha'Mivharim* (*The Book of Elections*). Cluj, Romania: 1939. (Hebrew)

Levin, Israel, ed. *Abraham Ibn Ezra - Reader: Annotated texts with introduction and commentaries*. Tel Aviv and New York: Israel Matz Publications, 1985. (Hebrew)

Levy, Raphael. *The Astrological Works of Abraham ibn Ezra – A literary and linguistic study with special reference to the Old*

French Translation of Hagin. Baltimore, MD: John Hopkins Press. 1927.

Levy, Tony and Charles Burnett. "Sefer ha-Middot: A Mid-Twelfth-Century Text on Arithmetic and Geometry Attributed to Abraham Ibn Ezra." *Aleph 6* (2006): 57-238.

Ptolemy, Claudius. *Tetrabiblos*. Translated by J. M. Ashmand. Chicago: Aries Press, 1933.

Sela, Shlomo and Gad Freudenthal. "Abraham Ibn Ezra's Scholarly Writings: A Chronological Listing." *Aleph 6* (2006): 13-55.

Smithuis, Renate. "Abraham Ibn Ezra's Astrological Works in Hebrew and Latin: New Discoveries and Exhaustive Listing." *Aleph 6* (2006): 239-338.

CPSIA information can be obtained at www.ICGtesting.com
Printed in the USA
BVOW07s0956091013

333291BV00001B/101/P